DR. WES ADAMS

M000032832

REVIVAL

Its Present Relevance
& Coming Role at the End of the Age

Revival: Its Present Relevance & Coming Role at the End of the Age
Copyright @ 2010
Published by Fusion Ministries, Inc.

John Wesley Adams and Rhonda Hughey
www.fusionministry.com

Cover Design by Ben Hoeppner
Layout Artist Dale Jimmo

Unless otherwise identified, Scripture quotations are from
the The Holy Bible New International Version 1973, 1978,
1984 by international Bible Society. Used by permission by
Zondervan Publishing House. All rights reserved.

Other Scripture quotations used are NKJV (the New King
James Version); NASB (New American Standard Bible); ESV
(English Standard Version); NLT (New Living Translation).

All rights reserved. No part of this publication may be re-
produced, stored in a retrieval system, or transmitted in any
form or by any means—electronic, mechanical, photocopy-
ing, recording, or otherwise—without the prior written permission of the publisher. The only exception is brief quotations in printed reviews.

Published by Fusion Ministries, Inc.
721 Main Street, Suite 105
Grandview, MO 64030

Printed in the United States of America

ISBN 9780982601846

Library of Congress Control Number: 2010939246

This book is dedicated to

Jane L. Adams

My beloved wife

Jane loved God and His Word passionately. She was a devoted wife and lovingly served me for 30 years in countless ways, including my speaking and writing ministry. Jane, who died October 18, 2010, will have an inheritance in the coming revival because of her decades of intercession for it. My precious wife now joins the great cloud of witnesses in God's presence.

Table of Contents

Table of Contents

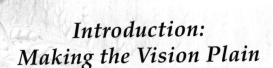

Introduction:
Making the Vision Plain

Write down the [vision] and make it plain . . . so that a herald may run
with it. For the [vision's fulfillment] awaits an appointed time;
it speaks of the end and will not prove false. Though it linger,
wait for it; it will certainly come and will not delay.

Habakkuk 2:2-3

I s there hope for revival in Western world nations in the 21st century or are the days of great revivals over? Overwhelming spiritual rebellion in Western culture abounds. Pervasive immorality, perversions, addictions, violence, disintegration of families, undaunted terrorist activity, sinister political maneuvering, economic instability, and hostile religions are threatening the church and society as we know it.

Are we beyond hope for revival or will there be another great revival as God's answer to the alarming increase of evil? In light of encroaching evil, many believers have lost hope that revival is still possible in our generation or that there will a great revival before the Lord returns?

Those in the earth who have been faithfully longing and interceding for revival need to be encouraged that they have not tied their soul to a dead-end dream. Revival is not only presently occurring in many places in the earth, there is yet coming a great, global revival before Jesus Christ returns. This book presents solid biblical and historical evidence that supports both of these assertions. We are not a people without hope!

The present generation desperately needs the revival vision to be written down and made plain so that they may run with it! This vision has past, present and future dimensions. This book will help the reader see the divine pattern in revival history, and understand what God is accomplishing in these great revivals as we move toward the omega point of redemption.

In this book we (1) present the larger redemptive context of past revival history (2) provide evidence of the present significance of revival among the nations in the 21st Century, and (3) reveal the characteristics of the coming great revival that will occur at the end of the age.

The meaning of history is not self-evident. All history has to be interpreted in order to be understood. This is true of revival history as well; past revival history begs to be interpreted. Understanding revival history through the lens of God's perspective enables us to see the larger patterns of His redemptive purpose the past 500 years.

Great revivals are not just a series of inspiring moments in history. They are intentional events that God has been using to move His church forward toward the culmination of redemption. In all things related to God, there is a larger picture and pattern that He is working on. It is impossible to gain this broad perspective by simply looking at our own context or generation.

The ancient Greeks viewed history as cyclical, always repeating itself, therefore going nowhere in particular, accomplishing no discernable purpose and without any identifiable goal. This philosophy of history is embraced by many modern historians and unfortunately by some in the church as well. We have been seduced by the spirit of the age and therefore we live for the moment without any understanding or concern for the past or the future.

For most people history seems to be one senseless crisis after another without any overarching purpose. This view creates frustration, futility and despair. Without a biblical perspective of history, we cannot know who we are, where we came from or where we are going. This leads to a hopeless, fearful and self-centered existence.

The biblical perspective of history, however, reveals God's redemptive purpose in history, thereby giving human history meaning, significance and direction. Jesus Christ is Lord of history! History began with Him (He was "before all things"—Col 1:17) and history (in this age) will end with Him. Jesus Christ is the alpha and omega of history. Christ transcends history as sovereign Lord and descends into history as the man Christ Jesus. If we want to know the meaning and outcome of history, we must look at what He has revealed in His Word concerning the culmination of redemption.

This book challenges the church to recognize her present hour of history and to prepare herself and the community where she lives for the approaching glory and manifest presence of God. In those places on the earth where God is pouring out His presence and power in revival, we find much hope. We see not just small breakthroughs but a manifestation of His kingdom on this side of eternity that is breath-taking!

As strategic as the present hour of history is, revivals occurring today in the nations today will pale in comparison to the final great revival that is yet ahead for the church! Biblical evidence indicates that the coming great revival will be global, and will challenge the dense darkness, revealing the great glory of our God. Jesus is coming as Bridegroom, King and Judge to rule in righteousness and justice over all the earth. The final revival will prepare the way for His return.

Complete fulfillment of the vision awaits faithful intercession and God's appointed time. The full vision *"speaks of the
end and will not prove false. Though it linger, wait for it; it will
certainly come and will not delay"* (Hab. 2:3). It's our prayer that
Jesus will be magnified as this book brings light regarding
God's present and end-time revival purposes for His church!

Part One

The Relevance of Great Revivals

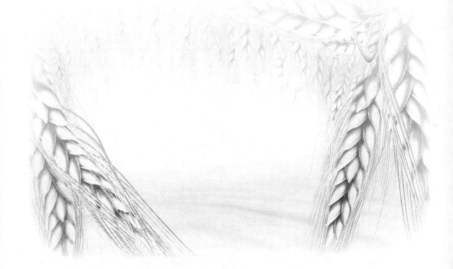

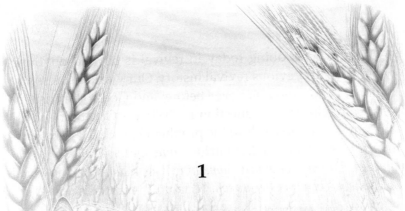

1

Great Revival or Terrible Judgment?

*"Look at the nations and watch—and be utterly amazed.
For I am going to do something in your days that
you would not believe, even if you were told."*

Habakkuk 1:5

Great revival is still a reality in the earth, and the greatest moment of revival impact is yet future. Likewise the judgments of God are still a reality in the earth, and the moment of greatest judgment is yet future. The greatest revival was not the Great Awakening; the greatest judgments were not the plagues of Egypt. The greatest revival and the most severe judgments of God will emerge simultaneously at the end of the age.

The perspective or mindset of many Christians about God and His ways at the end of the age is primarily based on other people's opinions, rather than on the authority of God's Word directly. Their understanding is restricted to seeing through one lens—their own sphere of interests and relationships.

Jesus modeled another way of "seeing" by focusing on what His Father was saying and doing. It is impossible to know fully what the Father is presently doing if we look only at the Bible through the lens of our own local church, denomination, or region. Jesus said, *"My Father is always working"* (John 5:17, NLT). Because He is *"always working,"* this means God is working now, not just in ancient biblical times.

7

What God is doing today in revival is beyond anything we've seen in previous revival history. Our world is presently a global community as never before; and God's story is emphatically global! The question is: "What is God doing globally now?" God's words to the prophet Habakkuk are instructive for us: *"Look at the nations and watch—and be utterly amazed. For I am going to do something in your days that you would not believe, even if you were told"* (Hab. 1:5, emphasis added).

This God-instruction could not be more contemporarily relevant! These words in Habakkuk challenge us to look beyond ourselves to what God is doing globally. When we look at what God is doing among the nations, we see His ways both in His judgments (cf. Hab. 1:6) and in great manifestations of His glory (cf. Hab. 2:14). Both are evident in the earth and both are speaking to us if we have eyes to see and ears to hear.

Two Opposite Tracks

Some leaders believe with conviction that there is *either* a great revival *or* terrible national judgment coming (as with Israel of old). The truth is what we are facing as a nation and as the world is not an either/or situation. A great revival is coming (if we humble ourselves and pray and seek God's face and turn from our wicked ways); *but also* dire judgments are coming according to God's Word. Great revival may yet postpone terrible judgment, but judgment seems more imminent in many places than revival. .

The spiritual state of the church in the Western world truly has placed it in great peril. One reason for this peril is God's presence has withdrawn to the point that biblical Christianity, spiritual life, moral conscience, evangelism, and church growth have shifted from the Western world to non-western nations. Major denominational leaders have so compromised with the decadence of Western culture that they now ordain practicing homosexuals as clergy and bishops. Church leaders of these same denominations in non-western nations so abhor the Western church's compromise, they are pulling away from their denomination's ecclesiastical structure. Need we be reminded that God gives a people or a nation over to judgment when these kinds of sins occur (Rom. 1:24-32)?

The Bible reveals that two opposite tracks will come to full ripeness at the end of the age. The Bible contrasts these two tracks in several different ways: good and evil, God's kingdom and Satan's kingdom, Christ and antichrist, the Bride and the harlot. Using still other biblical terms of contrast, there will be a full ripening of righteousness and wickedness, of the wheat and the tares. Certainly Satan will be doing his worst at the end of the age; but God also will be doing His best—bringing redemption to fullness and glorious culmination! It is not an issue of either terrible darkness or great light at the end of the age. Both of these realities will come to fullness. The fact is the Bible predicts at the end of the age both great global revival (Joel 2:28–32) and terrible global judgments (Ps. 110:6; Rev. 6:1–17; 8:7; 9:21; 16:1–21).

Billy Graham, in his address at the Lausanne Congress in 1974, summarized succinctly the hope we have as we await the climactic movement and the total fulfillment of what was done on the cross. Billy Graham referred to the future this way:

> I believe there are two strains in prophetic Scripture. One leads us to understand that as we approach the latter days and the Second Coming of Christ, things will become worse and worse. The Book of Joel speaks of *"multitudes, multitudes in the valley of decision!"* The day of the Lord is near in the valley of decision. **He is speaking of judgment.**
>
> But I believe as we approach the latter days and the coming of the Lord, **it could be a time also of great revival.** We cannot forget the possibility and the promise of revival, the refreshing of the latter days of the outpouring of the

> Spirit promised in Joel 2:28 and repeated in Acts 2:17. That
> will happen right up to the advent of the Lord Jesus Christ.
>
> **Evil will grow worse, but God will be mightily at work
> at the same time.** I am praying that we will see . . . the "lat-
> ter rains," a rain of blessings, showers falling from heaven
> upon all the continents before the coming of the Lord.

The Bible clearly reveals that our world is headed toward
catastrophic climax. Contemporary forces of evil are becoming more united in their sinister aggression against God. At
the same time there are increasing signs of an unprecedented
spiritual awakening worldwide. Never has there been more
yearning by more people for more spiritual reality. Nor has
the church ever had the means it now has to proclaim the gospel of the kingdom to the whole world as a testimony to all
nations.

The Nations – Judgment!
He is the LORD our God;
his judgments are in all the earth.
Psalm 105:7

One thing we see when we look around us is a great increase of evil and darkness as the Bible predicts will occur in
the end-time. The Bible teaches that when history reaches its
fullness of time preceding Jesus' second coming, there will be
an enormous clash between Satan's kingdom of darkness and
God's kingdom of light. The magnitude of this clash will be
unprecedented as evil approaches its cumulative fullness on
the earth and as redemption approaches its cumulative fullness at the same time.

As is often true in biblical prophecy, God's Word has multiple levels of fulfillment. Habakkuk 1:5 – *"For I am going to do
something in your days that you would not believe, even if you were
told"* – has at least three levels of prophetic application. First,
it has an *immediate*, short-range application in the lifetime of

the prophet. Second, it has a *future* application and fulfillment in connection with the first coming of Christ and the ministry of the Early Church (Acts 13:40–48). Third, it will have a cumulative future fulfillment on a grand scale during the generation to which the Lord Jesus returns. This fulfillment will involve both global displays of God's judgments and global displays of God's glory.

The immediate application of 1:5 in Habakkuk's day concerned terrifying judgment for Jerusalem and his whole nation. God revealed to Habakkuk that the much feared Babylonians would be His instrument of judgment against Judah and Jerusalem. The Babylonians were invading one nation after another—conquering, pillaging, and destroying cities. Because Jerusalem had broken covenant with God and had persisted in her unrepentant sin as the nation's capital, she too would soon fall. Jerusalem—the city of David and of the Holy Temple built by Solomon and the home of many prophets— was soon to be severely judged by God.

Habakkuk was horrified! Wasn't Jerusalem a city and Judah a nation that God had raised up, favored and greatly blessed? Hadn't they experienced God's glory in their history? Hadn't He protected them from the enemy before? Why was God now sending an enemy to devastate those He had previously blessed with His presence and glory?

Prophets like Isaiah, Micah and Jeremiah had warned Judah for many years about impending judgment if she did not repent of her idolatry, immorality, bloodshed, and broken covenant. God was unmistakably clear in His warnings and was merciful in His delays—now judgment was at the door. The *God who judges in the earth* (Ps. 58:11 NKJV) was now at the door to judge the nation of Abraham and Moses, and the City of David. Unthinkable? Yes, but now a tragic fact of history!

Shortly after God's word to Habakkuk, the ruthless Babylonian army invaded Jerusalem three times (605 BC, 597 BC, and 586 BC). The final invasion was broad scaled. The invaders burned the Temple in Jerusalem, totally destroyed the city, and took almost all surviving Jewish inhabitants into captivity. The entire nation was left in devastation and ruin. The unthinkable did happen!

God always warns His people of impending judgment! When in the twenty-first century we "look at the nations," we see warning signs everywhere. We see the antichrist spirit rising up all over the world, manifesting itself in vicious hatred of the Jews and of faithful Christians who are loyal to Jesus as the only way to God (John 14:6; Acts 4:12). The antichrist spirit hates biblical truth and biblical moral standards. The central biblical truth that Jesus is the God-man and the only way to God the Father is already offensive—to mainstream Christianity, to politically-correct people, to secular society, and to all other religions. Antagonism toward the gospel is increasing rapidly!

As the kingdom of darkness and the spirit of antichrist is expanding its base politically and economically—planning its global strategy, and waiting for its opportune hour at the end of the age—many in the Western church are in deep spiritual slumber and deception.

The Bible is unmistakably clear that there will be great deception and a great falling away at the end. Spirituality will be popular, but it will not be Jesus-centered nor based on biblical revelation. The Bible makes clear that the end-time judgments of God will be poured out on an antichrist world given over to the lust of the flesh, the lust of the eyes, and an arrogant rejection of Jesus Christ.

The Nations — Revival!
Let Your glory be above all the earth.
Psalm 57:11 (NKJV)

As the Lord brings redemptive history to a grand culmination at the end of the age, a final global revival is indicated in

Scripture. This great outpouring will make possible a vast spiritual harvest of lost humanity, restore widespread awareness of God and His glory, magnify the name of Jesus in the earth, and prepare a pure and spotless Bride for the Bridegroom.

This means a great revival is still ahead of us! We presently have the privilege of partnering with God the Father in the final preparation of the ages for great revival and the coming again of the Lord Jesus.

Because the Bible predicts a great increase of evil and darkness in the end-time, many Christians mistakenly believe there will be no end-time revival. As a result, many of these believers are unaware of what God is doing. They are unable to look at the nations and be amazed at the *present surge in redemption* occurring worldwide. They are unable to consider and appreciate the amazing miracles of transformation that are occurring currently and increasing among the nations.

How can we know there will be a final great revival at the end of the age? What is the biblical evidence that points to such a revival before Christ returns? The Old Testament prophet Joel answers this question in three ways.

First, Joel affirms that there will be an end-time revival in the form of a global outpouring of the Spirit on *"all people"* (Joel 2:28–29). When this happens, Joel says—that among the "all people"—*"everyone who calls on the name of the Lord will be saved"* (*Joel 2:32a*). *This biblical prophecy does not say "all people"* will be saved, but rather that everyone will have the opportunity to call on the name of the Lord and be saved. This indicates that in the last great outpouring, salvation will be happening globally—on "all people," presently approaching 7 billion people and growing. The grand finale will be on a massive scale!

Second, another aspect of this promise by the prophet Joel and repeated by the apostle Peter, is now beginning to happen—namely the global outpouring of the Holy Spirit. This outpouring is to happen especially [not exclusively] to sons and daughters and young men and young women, who will prophesy and faithfully carry the testimony of Jesus in the earth (Joel 2:28–29; Acts 2:17; cf. Rev. 19:10). Today *the strength* of the global missions' movement and the global prayer movement is the present large numbers of youth or young adults in them. Spirit-filled young men and women are predicted to be prominent on the frontlines prophesying—and this is increasingly happening in this generation.

Third, Joel speaks of the fullness of the final revival as a global outpouring of the Spirit in the context of unfolding eschatological signs at the very end of the age (Joel 2:30–31). While other biblical evidence strongly supports a great endtime revival as well (see Chapter 12), the strongest and most indisputable biblical evidence is found in Joel's prophecy about a global outpouring of the Holy Spirit *when* eschatological signs in the heavens and on the earth are occurring. These very same eschatological signs are described in the New Testament as happening in connection with the time of Jesus' return (see Matt., Mark, Luke, and Rev.).

Consistent with Joel's prophecy of a global outpouring at the very end, is the prophecy in Revelation 7:9, 14, about a massive worldwide harvest involving all nations, tribes, people, and languages (Rev. 7:9). This enormous end-time harvest will come at a time of great end-time trouble (Rev. 7:14). *Historically*, great harvests of salvation since AD 1500 have always occurred in the context of great revivals. *Logically and exegetically*, the final end-time harvest will be the result of the final great revival and spiritual awakening foreseen in Joel 2.

When Habakkuk prophesied that *"the earth will be filled with the knowledge of the glory of the LORD,"* he placed the 2:14 promise not in a tranquil context, but rather in the midst of five "woe" judgments of God in the earth (Hab. 2:6, 9, 12, 15, 19). Habakkuk thus indicates that the earth will be filled with awareness of God's glory in troubled times of "woe."

What will the full ripening of good and evil look like? Among other things, true believers will be lovers of truth and lovers of God in the midst of those who are lovers of sinful pleasure and haters of God. True believers will stand out in contrast to all other religions, as did the early church in the polytheistic Roman world of the first century. A massive harvest of true salvation and radical disciples will occur in contrast to and in conflict with a hostile global-ecumenical-religious movement that will be politically correct and fully aligned with the world's system.

Although we see dark clouds of judgment gathering in our world, we also see something else – the glory of God being manifested in unprecedented ways in transforming revival! Clearly God is now at work globally to magnify His Son and put on display the full victory of the slain Lamb.

The Bible declares that when God's glory is most openly manifested, it will be dramatically visible against the back-drop of "thick darkness" (Isa. 60:1–3; cf. Rev. 11:6–7). Whereas the initial fulfillment of Isaiah 60 was when Jesus began His ministry in Galilee (Matt. 4:12–17), the full realization of Isaiah 60 will be on the threshold of Jesus' return (Rev. 7:9, 14).

Surely, we are now witnessing the beginning of the eschatological fulfillment of Isaiah 60 in the growing confrontation globally between light and darkness, between God's kingdom and Satan's, as the ultimate collision occurs in the end-time culmination of this present age.

Is there indication of God's glory being openly manifested today in the midst of encroaching darkness? Yes! In the midst of ugly wars, persistent poverty, and unspeakable natural and human devastation, we look among the nations and are utterly amazed by what we see. Hundreds and hundreds of communities worldwide are experiencing supernatural transformation on a scale never before seen in church history!

There Is Hope!

In addition to impending judgment, God emphatically promised Habakkuk that a time was coming when *"the earth will be filled with the knowledge of the glory of the LORD, as the waters cover the sea"* (Hab. 2:14). God knows, and Habakkuk came to see, that the message of judgment by itself causes people to lose hope. God's people always need the full perspective of what God is doing in their generation and beyond. The foremost longing in God's heart is not judgment, but rather the global manifestation of His glory!

God always seeks to fill His people with hope, and with all joy, and peace in believing, so that His chosen ones may *"abound in hope"* (NKJV) [*"overflow with hope"* (NIV)] *by the power of the Holy Spirit* (Ro 15:13). The New Testament speaks of *"Christ in [us]"* being *"the hope of glory"* (Col. 1:27). The gospel is inherently filled with the message and reality of hope.

A world without spiritual light and hope is a dark place of devastation and chaos. Without Jesus Christ, man is without God and without hope in the world (Eph. 2:12). Because of Jesus, however, there is perpetual hope! *Revival from heaven* is the revelation of Jesus as heaven's light and glory suddenly bursting forth in corporate manifestation on the earth in a community, region, or nation. *Revival from heaven* is God's kingdom and will be ("as it is in heaven") coming to earth in powerful manifestation.

Is there hope for the Western church in a culture that has become humanistic, secular, morally corrupt, scoffers of God? The church's main concern is to "fit-in" and "be contemporary." Will the church be overcome by her increasing compromise with darkness and depravity in the end? The compromising, backslidden, unbelieving, and humanistic Western church will be swallowed up by the one-world religion in the end (called "the great harlot" in Rev. 17).

But the blood-washed, faithful, God-fearing, worshiping, praying, passionate, and global Bride of Christ will be victorious and see the light of the glory of God in this century! The showdown has begun! Wisdom says choose today which side you're going to be on, for your choices today will determine your allegiance tomorrow. Anti-God and anti-Christ evil will never be too ominous and oppressive worldwide for there not to be a final great global display of God's power and salvation on the earth before Jesus returns!

The church of the Lord Jesus Christ has an important role to play in this unfolding drama of the ages and we must understand what God is doing now so we can partner with Him in *His story*. In redemption's unfolding story the past 500 years, God has used revival as the great catalyst to move the church forward toward the fullness of His redemptive purposes. He again will and is using revival to bring redemption to fullness in this age.

Why Faith Is Necessary

All of God's promises must be pursued and possessed by faith. Faith is active, never passive, and requires us to believe the promise before it becomes tangible reality. The principle is—*"the promise comes by faith, so that it may be by grace"* (Rom. 4:16). During the interim between promise and fulfillment, faith must focus on *"the God who gives life to the dead and calls things that are not as though they were"* (Rom. 4:17). The challenge that faith always faces is the same as that of Abraham:

> *Against all hope, Abraham in hope believed. . . . Without weakening in his faith, he faced the fact that his body was as good as dead. . . . Yet he did not waver through unbelief regarding the promise of God, but was strengthened in his faith and gave glory to God, being fully persuaded that God had power to do what he had promised* (Rom. 4:18–21).

Faith stretches us because faith relates to *things hoped for* and *to things not seen* (Heb. 11:1, NKJV). "Things hoped for" refer to those things that God has promised in His Word; "things not seen" refer to both the invisible spiritual realm and to things yet future.

Satan constantly challenges believers on both of these issues. Concerning God's promises, Satan intrudes with the thought, *"has God said?"* Concerning things promised but not yet fulfilled, Satan comes with unbelief that states: *"that will not come to pass!"* God is doing things in our day that many people will not believe—if they live in the Western world—even though they are well documented.

When the skeptical Sadducees tried to trap Jesus with a biblical question, *Jesus replied, "You are in error because you do not know the Scriptures or the power of God"* (Matt. 22:29). We err as Christians concerning faith most often for these same two reasons—we don't really know the Scriptures, and we don't really believe that the power of God is available today.

The Sadducees were the Jewish priests in Jesus' day (the professional clergy). The Pharisees and Scribes in Jesus' day were the foremost interpreters of Scripture (the biblical scholars).These professional clergy and biblical scholars did not understand the Scriptures correctly or perceive God's intended message. Consequently they erred greatly concerning the Scriptures and did not recognize Jesus, as their Messiah, foretold in the Old Testament.

These same Jewish clergymen and biblical scholars had refused to be baptized by John the Baptist. Because of their arrogance (according to Jesus), they *"rejected God's purpose for themselves, because they had not been baptized by John"* (Luke 7:29–30).

Paul was a Pharisee and a zealous Jewish Rabbi who did not "know" either the Scriptures (although highly trained in them) or the power of God (although religiously devout). He did not know what God was doing in his generation until his Damascus Road encounter with Jesus. During the next three years, the Spirit of wisdom and revelation so filled and transformed his mind that he could then see clearly what God was doing in his generation.

When the first century Jews saw multitudes of Gentiles hearing and responding in faith to the gospel, they were "filled with envy," opposed Paul, and rejected his message. Even though God was doing an amazing and miraculous work in their day, and though it was being declared openly to them by apostolic messengers, they chose not to believe or accept the good work God was doing (Acts 13:40–42, 44–46, 48, NKJV).

In this context Paul quotes Habakkuk 1:5 and applies it to the redemption and transformation that Jesus was and is bringing to the nations through apostolic preaching and by the power of the Holy Spirit (Acts 13:40–48). Paul quoted Habakkuk 1:5 to a Jewish audience in a Gentile city when preaching Jesus as their promised Messiah. In response to the unbelief expressed by many in his Jewish audience, Paul warned them as follows:

> *Beware therefore, lest what has been spoken in the prophets*
> *come upon you: 'Behold, you despisers, Marvel and perish!*
> *For I will work a work in your days,*
> *A work which you will by no means believe,*
> *Though one were to declare it to you* (Acts 13:40–41 NKJV).

This scene recurs throughout church history! The pattern is when God is doing a new thing in the earth, most religious people either refuse to take notice or refuse to believe. Most religious Jews in Paul's day refused even to consider—much less believe— the evidence he was presenting to them about Jesus as Messiah.

In Western cultures most believers are educated in a anti-supernatural, humanistic worldview. They are taught to analyze according to the natural mind. Natural reasoning then overrides the functioning of the spirit faculty to discern truth and dulls the capacity for seeing, believing, and understanding the spiritual realm in which God lives and works. If God were speaking to us today, as He did to Habakkuk, surely He would say to us: *"You will not believe, even if you were told, what I am doing in your day"* (Hab. 1:5, paraphrased). If unbelief is a major stronghold in us, God will pass us by—*"because we didn't recognize the time of His great visitation for us"* (cf. Luke 19:44, paraphrased).

This is a time to actively agree with God's report about what He is doing elsewhere and to actively intercede for the fullness of what God has promised but we haven't yet seen. When we contend for something we haven't seen, even if there is frustration in our crying out, this can become the travail of soul—like that of Hannah—that gives birth to the fulfillment of God's prophetic promises.

As God's people, we seriously need the full perspective of what God is doing now among the nations. God is holy and His righteous judgments are in the earth. But the foremost longing in God's heart is mercy, not judgment; it is revival and the manifestation of His glory, not devastation and destruction! Clearly God is now at work globally to magnify His Son and put on display the full victory of the cross in the midst of troubled times.

2

What Is Revival from Heaven?

*"LORD, I have heard of your fame; I stand in awe of your deeds,
LORD repeat them in our day, in our time make them
known; in wrath remember mercy."* Habakuk 3:2

Revival from heaven is the holy manifestation of God's presence descending on the church. Revival restores the activity of the Holy Spirit, His gifts and His power to the church—accompanied by an extraordinary burden of prayer, public confession of sin, and exceedingly great joy!

When great revival from heaven occurs, the fire of God's Spirit descends from heaven and sweeps through society like a cleansing flame. What does this look like? Revival from heaven is:

> When men in the streets are afraid to speak godless words for fear that God's judgment will fall! When sinners, aware of the fire of God's presence, tremble in the streets and cry out for mercy! When (without human advertising) the Holy Spirit sweeps across cities and regions in supernatural power and holds people in the grip of terrifying conviction! When every store becomes a pulpit, every heart an altar, every home a sanctuary, and people walk carefully before God! This, my beloved, is truly RE-VIVAL *FROM HEAVEN!*[1]

Robert Coleman describes great revival as "some measure of heaven coming down to earth." As a result, "men and women with lives devastated by sin find in Jesus the grace to repent and the power to change. Wrongs are made right. Broken homes reunite. The church, made beautiful in holiness, reaches out in love to serve a hurting and lost world."[2]

Revival from heaven is vastly different from inspiring church services, a week of "revival services," special conferences, or evangelistic campaigns. In these kinds of corporate gatherings, thousands may be inspired and edified; people may be brought to a saving knowledge of Jesus Christ and the local church may experience God's refreshing—for which we thank God. But let's not mistake these events for revival from heaven. After these events occur—as far as the community, city or region is concerned—little measurable impact happens. Sin, crime, godlessness, and secular humanism continue to devastate all levels of society unabated as darkness continues to advance.

Unlike a personal or local church revival, *revival from heaven is a revival that impacts society*. Classic revival begins when a city, region, or nation experience the heavens opening above them as a result of intercession and spiritual preparation. Subsequently, the Holy Spirit descends from the throne of God in power in response to a humble, waiting, contrite, and praying people.

J. Edwin Orr (1912–1987) believes *great revival is a direct consequence of **a geographical outpouring of the Holy Spirit***. The great revival begins when a city, region, or nation experiences the heavens opening above and the Holy Spirit descending in power from God's throne of governance.

- Revival in the church is one consequence of such an outpouring.
- Spiritual awakening in society is the other consequence.[3]

Both consequences begin with an outpouring of the Holy

Spirit from heaven that is *geographical* and *experiential*.

By *geographical* we mean the outpouring is in a specific geographical area. It may be local as in one community, or it may cover a larger region such as a county, state, nation, or even spread to nations. But the epicenter is geographically specific.

By *experiential* we mean the presence and power of the Holy Spirit results in spiritual awakening. Spiritual awakening is a widespread God-consciousness among saints and sinners alike that produces an extraordinary conviction [for] sin, fear of God and His judgment, confession and repentance of sin. People in society are experiencing God's love, mercy, and forgiveness, and having life-changing encounters with Him.

Defining "Revival"

Classic revival from heaven is a redemptive phenomenon that has appeared largely since the Reformation (AD 1500). Although there were occasional pockets of revival and renewal in early Christianity and the middle ages, classic revivals are a divine-human phenomenon that uniquely characterizes church history since the Reformation.

How are we to understand the word "revival"? Revival—by dictionary definition—means to reanimate, to renew, to awaken, to invigorate with life, to restore to new life, that which is lethargic or asleep, dying or dead.

What is revival from heaven? Revival from heaven is revival that impacts both the church and society! There is an acute awareness of God and His holiness that changes the spiritual climate of a whole community or region. This may also be called a "spiritual awakening." Spiritual awakening in society is accompanied by an extraordinary conviction for sin, fear of God and His judgment, revelation of God's love and mercy, confession and repentance of sin, and people inquiring—as on the Day of Pentecost— "what must I do to be saved?"

Revival from heaven involves spiritual rain from heaven—i.e., an outpouring of the Holy Spirit on the collective people of God that revives the church and awakens the society where it occurs. Revivals from heaven are supernatural days when God openly manifests His presence in overwhelming reality.

Authentic revival from heaven leaves the saint and sinner alike with a profound awareness of God's greatness and transcendence, and of their own sinfulness and need of Him. [4]

J. Edwin Orr, the foremost historian of great revivals, defines revival from heaven as "a movement of the Holy Spirit that brings about a revival of New Testament Christianity in the church and spiritual awakening in its related community."[5]

Why Is Revival Necessary?

Revival from heaven is necessary because it is *God's way* of counteracting the recurring problem of spiritual and moral decline in the church. There is a physical law called "The Second Law of Thermodynamics" that illustrates the similar spiritual problem recurring in the church.

"The Second Law of Thermodynamics" is a law or principle in physics which states that energy and matter in the physical realm naturally tend to run down, not up; naturally move from order toward chaos; naturally degenerate from harmonious complexity to random disorder. "The Second Law" means that the energy of a system loses momentum and eventually takes the form or structure of a lesser type. The measure of this physical disorder is called *entropy*.

The Bible reveals that physical, spiritual, and moral entropy was introduced to the human race and the created order through the sin and fall of Adam. Without the intervention of God's grace and power, the direction of things physically, spiritually and morally is downward, not upward; everything moves toward decline, decay, and death apart from God's intervention.

For this reason and others, the power and influence of great revivals seldom endure more than one generation before they lose momentum and decline. *Revival is God's way of countering the operation of "The Second Law of Thermodynamics" in the spiritual realm.* Revival from heaven is God's redemptive intervention in the spiritual and moral spheres, sometimes even in the physical realm, for His honor, praise, glory, and redemptive plan. Thus, classic revivals have always been times of upward and forward progress in the church and society.

Who Is Responsible for Revival?

Revival from heaven is always attributable to God in origin and initiative. Revival is God's idea and design; He is "the grand architect"[6] of all great revivals and spiritual awakenings. But as in all things Christian, God is the initiator and humans are the responders. In this sense, revival is a divine and human partnership!

Since revivals are an open manifestation of God's presence corporately and usually involve "a suddenly from heaven" visitation, the sovereign element of God is always a part of the mystery of revival. Sovereignty is God's ability to transcend all human contingencies in order to bring forth His kingdom as a redemptive tapestry. The outcome of revival depends not on man's clever wisdom or strategy, but rather on God's manifest presence and power.

God clearly plans His own visits! His visitations come, however, in response to man's wholehearted preparation. We know from observation that God is especially attracted to an environment of humility and brokenness (not ambition and strength), desperate spiritual hunger, repentance and obedience, and urgent and united intercessory prayer. God comes when the human factor reaches a spiritual critical mass as God sees it in His wisdom and strategy.

Revivals are thus a joint venture between God and His

people. We are not to wait for revival *passively*—as if God chooses to visit some communities randomly and we "hope" that He will choose to visit our church or community also.

Passivity was the prevailing attitude of the church when William Carey (1761–1834) was called by God to leave his homeland (England) to go as a missionary to India. His opponents argued, "If God wants to save the heathen, He will do it without us." Many view revival the same way. Their attitude is, "If God wants to send revival, He will sovereignly do so without our preparation and prevailing prayer."

The testimony of history, however, is to the contrary. God always partners with His people to bring about redemption on the earth. Oftentimes, as with Gideon's 30,000 volunteers, God reduces our numbers and assets so that we don't boast about our strength in the day of His visitation and power.

Man has a tendency to think he can pull it off with some prayer, planning, finances, or resources! Therefore, God often reduces our strength and numbers so that it is seen to be His strength, not ours, that saves and transforms a city. God's weakness is stronger than man's strength. God chooses the weak things of the world to shame the strong "so that no one may boast before Him" (1 Cor. 1:29).[7]

It is an observable fact of church history that God chooses to visit those people who are truly humble and who are most spiritually hungry for Him. *Revival happens only when our hunger for God's presence trumps all earth-bound desires and appetites.* Moreover, God has a special love for the humble! God chooses to dwell with the lowly and humble and contrite of heart. God derives pleasure and comfort from being in the presence of a humble people whose preeminent hunger is for His presence.

How Long Does Revival Last?

Historical observation tells us that revivals vary in their duration. However, a huge question about revival remains about its length: "When revival comes, how can we sustain it?" What are some basic principles required for seeing revival last for more than one to three years?

First, it is important to understand that there are *three basic phases* in a revival:

- the preparation phase,
- God's visitation phase (the most intense part of revival),
- the transformational impact phase.

When we think of revival, we tend to think primarily or exclusively of the visitation phase. The greatest visitation of God that the earth has ever known was when God came in the incarnation of His Son, Jesus Christ. Although Jesus' life on the earth was 33 years, His public ministry was only about three years in duration. Interestingly however, the visitation phase of many revivals has lasted only about three years. In fact, the three most influential twentieth century revivals— Welsh Revival (1904–1906), Azusa Street Revival (1906–1909), and Hebrides Revival (1949-1952), lasted just three years in their visitation stage.

The impact and multiplication of revival, however, can last for many years and decades with continuing fruit and ongoing influence. The clearest example of a long-lasting classic revival was the English revival led by John Wesley (1703–1791). The Wesleyan Revival in eighteenth century England continued effectively for sixty years after the initial revival visitation because John Wesley saw beyond the immediate excitement of the revival phenomena that was occurring and prepared for the future.

The genius of John Wesley as a revivalist lay in the fact that he was also a gifted teacher and an apostolic leader with a wise building strategy. Wesley wanted to see the impact and fruit of revival preserved and extended even beyond his own lifetime. Therefore, Wesley developed a new wineskin during the transformational phase of revival that focused on discipling converts and multiplication.

More specifically, the new wineskin Wesley created was a spiritual authority structure that involved training leaders and developing a network of small groups for spiritual nourishing and personal accountability of the converts. The revival and new wineskin combination was so effective that it birthed the Methodist Church worldwide.

If *the third phase of revival* is neglected or ignored, the revival will be shorter-lived than God intends. The duration of a great revival is determined by the level of preparation that precedes it, by the impact of the visitation that comes, by the wisdom of the leaders who steward it and by the purpose of God that sustains it.

Preparation and foresight help lay *the foundation for revival*, help perpetuate the revival when it comes, and can help reproduce and multiply the fruit of revival! The fruit of great revival is transformation that has in its foundation biblical principles and Jesus' kingdom value system. Biblical principles and Jesus' kingdom values provide a solid foundation for harvesting the fruit of revival, maintaining a high level of spiritual life in a community, and providing an ongoing resting place for God's manifest presence.

This foundational understanding allows the spiritual DNA of revival to be intentionally perpetuated. A revival's duration and lasting fruitfulness is clearly determined in part by whether the revival has a biblical and principle-based foundation, or whether the revival lacks biblical foundation and is primarily a burst of life and spiritual energy that more quickly dissipates and passes.

Finally, the *spiritual appetites and disciplines* that initially attracted the fire of God in a revival visitation are the very same appetites and disciplines God uses to sustain and lengthen the revival's duration with resulting fruit. During a revival spiritual leaders must remain humble and obedient, treasure and honor God's presence, quickly repent of all sin, be intentionally devoted to prayer and intimacy with God, and continually long for more of God and His resting presence as the highest priority.

The nature and degree of our ongoing appetite for God will be directly related to how long God stays once He arrives. Just as fervent prayer must precede a revival visitation, so the presence of the Holy Spirit and the power of prayer and intimacy with God must undergird and sustain revival when it comes.

A Glimpse of Revival from Heaven

One of the least impressive revival settings but perhaps the greatest revival outcomes is the Azusa Street Revival. The revival began in Los Angeles in the spring of 1906 in an unpainted mule barn, formerly a humble Methodist church—truly a "Bethlehem stable setting."

The foremost leader was a humble black man who was blind in one eye. The seating was constructed from small barrels and lumber planks. Everything about the circumstances was offensive to the natural mind including "speaking in tongues" and "prophesying." The church culture in Los Angeles and beyond was not ready for this spiritual revolution and soon to be global revival. What were the services like? Here is a brief glimpse of this revival—the Azusa Street Revival—at the "Apostolic Faith Mission" in 1906.

> The services ran almost continuously. Seeking souls
> could be found under the power almost any hour, night

and day. The place was never closed nor empty. The people came to meet God. He was always there. Hence a continuous meeting. The meeting did not depend on the human leader. God's presence became more and more wonderful. In that old building, with its low rafters and bare floors, God took strong men and women to pieces and put them together again for His glory. Pride and self-assertion, self-importance and self-esteem, could not survive there. The religious ego preached its own funeral quickly.

. . . We had no prearranged program to be jammed through on time. Our time was the Lord's. We had real testimonies, from fresh heart experience. A dozen might be on their feet at one time, trembling under the mighty power of God.

. . . We were shut up to God in prayer in the meetings, our minds on Him. . . . We thought only of obeying God. In fact, there was an atmosphere of God there that forbade anyone but a fool attempting to put himself forward without the real anointing. And such did not last long. The meetings were controlled by the Spirit, from the throne.. . . God himself would give the altar call. Men would fall all over the house, like the slain in battle, or rush for the altar en masse, to seek God. The scene often resembled a forest of fallen trees. Such a scene cannot be imitated.

I never saw an altar call given in those early days. God himself would call them.. . . The whole place was steeped in prayer. God was in His holy temple. It was for man to keep silent. The Shekinah glory rested there. In fact, some claim to have seen the glory by night over the building. I do not doubt it. I have stopped more than once within two blocks of the place and prayed for strength before I dared go on. The presence of the Lord was so real. We saw some wonderful things in those days. Even very good men came to abhor themselves in the clearer light of God. The preachers died the hardest. They had so much to die to. So much reputation and good works. But when God got through with them, they gladly turned a new page and chapter. [8]

One of Jesus' very hard statements is—*"that which is highly esteemed among men is detestable in the sight of God"* (Luke 16:15 NASB). The converse is also often true, that which God highly esteems is detestable in the sight of men. The church world for the most part despised Azusa Street Revival but not God! If a revival is judged by the quality and quantity of fruit produced, then Azusa Street was the greatest catalytic revival of all time. But God is ready to do yet another new thing in the earth—unto fullness! What will it look like?

3

Timeless Features of Great Revival

Oh, that you would rend the heavens and come down,
that the mountains would tremble before you!
As when fire sets twigs ablaze and causes water to boil,
come down to make your name known to your enemies
and cause the nations to quake before you!

Isaiah 64:1–2

There are certain revival features that are timeless and always characterize great revivals. This chapter highlights twelve of these timeless revival features. They help us understand God and His ways as revealed in revival history, including greater revelation about His nature and character. Understanding God's ways and character helps bring the church into agreement with Him— the first critical step forward on the road to revival.

12 Timeless Features of Great Revival

1. Revival is Mysterious!

Revival is not mysterious in the preparation required for it, but there is a mysterious element about God's revival visitation. Revival visitation is mysterious like the wind. We cannot see the wind, we can only see the effects or manifestations of the wind. Revival is difficult to see by the natural mind, but the various manifestations and fruit of revival are visible.

No two great revival visitations by God are exactly the same. Revival has been likened unto waves. Waves can be as small as a ripple from a pebble thrown into a lake or as large as a huge breaker-wave crashing in from the ocean onto land.

Because God is infinite in His being, clothed in light and shrouded in mystery—and because great revival is a visitation of God's presence and light—revival bears God's own hallmark. Just as there is a mysterious dimension to God, so also there is to revival. God cannot be fully explained, neither can revival from heaven be fully grasped. Neither God nor His revival visitation can be reduced to finite reasoning. As one writer observes:

> Could [we] succeed in doing so, it would probably leave [us] disappointed and disillusioned. The mystery is part of the wonder, and when we lose the sense of wonder we lose the sense of worship. We are not permitted to probe into the secret things that belong to God, but we are to acquaint ourselves with the things that are revealed, for they belong to us and to our children.[1]

2. Revival is Exhilarating!

Joy, praise, and singing are always contagiously and powerfully present in times of great revival. Earle E. Cairns notes that most of the great evangelical songs and hymns of the church were inspired and written during times of revival. They express the joyful response of the soul concerning profound truth about God and subjective experience of spiritual realities recovered because of revival.[2]

Martyn Lloyd-Jones (1899–1981), in his book *Preaching and Preachers* states that nothing in his own experience has been more exhilarating and helpful than reading about the history of revivals. Why? One sees the footprint of God more clearly defined in classic revival history than in any other facet of history since biblical times. Reading about great revivals, their leaders and their societal impact is not only inspiring, but also insightful concerning God's ongoing involvement in human history. It raises one's perspective above the depressing bad news in public media and builds one's faith in God and His Lordship over history and its outcome.

If recounting or reading about historic revivals of the past is exhilarating to the believer's mind and spirit, think what the actual living experience of authentic revival would be like. In the natural realm of God's creation, hiking in the mountains or standing on the shoreline of a mighty ocean is an especially exhilarating experience. Revival is that kind of exhilarating, invigorating, and enlarging experience in the spiritual realm— a mountaintop place in God's story.

3. Revival is Jesus-Centered!

Some measure of the life, simplicity, and fervor of the early church's love and devotion to Jesus is always restored in great revival. Yes, true revival always recovers pure devotion to Jesus! Why? Because great revival restores the centrality of Jesus, a Christ-centered life, and a contagious testimony of Jesus.

Insofar as great revival is an outpouring of the Holy Spirit and because the Spirit's foremost ministry is to glorify Christ and make Him known, revival is necessarily Christ-centered. Any "revival" that is possible without the Lord Jesus Christ is a "revival" of a different kind of spirit than the Spirit of Christ (1 John 4:1–3).[3]

During Paul's three year ministry at Ephesus, the Holy Spirit was prominent and empowered Paul's persuasive proclamation of the kingdom of God. As a result, *all the Jews and Greeks who lived in the province of Asia heard the word of the Lord* (Acts 19:10). Acts 19 continues that all those living in Ephesus were seized with the fear of God, *and the name of the Lord Jesus was held in high honor* (v. 17). The New King James Version reads, *the name of the Lord Jesus was being magnified.*

In great revival, the name of the Lord Jesus is magnified and His name becomes the most revered name in the community or region. In revival the Holy Spirit magnifies the New Testament Jesus:

- what He has done in the finished work of the cross,
- the power of His resurrection,
- His ongoing ministry as our High Priest in heaven,
- the authority of His name and Lordship,
- the meaning of His kingdom,
- the urgency of His Great Commission, and
- the certainty of His Second Coming as the Bridegroom, King, and Judge.

Burns observes that Unitarianism, deism, cults, and all forms of biblical and theological liberalism (which reject Jesus' full deity, and the cross and blood of Jesus as the only basis of our salvation) know nothing about revival. Such movements cannot experience revival since there is nothing to revive. Their only hope is to repent, believe the gospel, and be saved through faith in Christ alone like all other sinners.

4. Revival Challenges the Status Quo

Authentic revival will interrupt church schedules, expose the shallowness of church programs, and turn man-centered Christianity upside-down. When it comes, revival will disturb leaders who are comfortable in their church nest. In every way imaginable, revival disrupts the church's status quo! James Burns describes this element of revival:

> It comes to scorch before it heals; it comes to condemn ministers and people for their unfaithful witness, for their

> selfish living, for their neglect of the cross, and to call them to daily renunciation, to an evangelical poverty, and to a deep and daily consecration.
>
> This is why a revival has ever been unpopular with large numbers within the church. Because it says nothing to them of [ecclesiastical position or]power such as they have learned to love, or of ease, or of success; it accuses them of sin, it tells them that they are dead, it calls them to awake, to renounce the world, and to follow Christ. [4]

This is why the compromised and lukewarm Western church generally is uninterested in revival. Many church leaders and influential people arrogantly disdain it as—irrelevant, not worthy of their crowded schedule and a carryover of an outdated mindset. Revival will always challenge and upset the status quo!

5. Revival Changes the Spiritual Atmosphere!

When the heavens are opened and God pours out His Spirit, a change in the spiritual atmosphere happens in a community or region. Duncan Campbell (1898–1972) spoke of the Hebrides Revival as *a community saturated with God*.[5] In that revival the manifest presence of God was everywhere, an inescapable fact—in homes, the marketplace, churches, places of entertainment, and by the roadside—and thus changing the spiritual climate. Many who visited the Isle of Lewis during the Hebrides' revival "became vividly conscious of the spiritual atmosphere before they reached the island." The public awareness of God's presence and holiness (initially strongest on the island of Lewis) then spread to other islands. This change in the spiritual atmosphere in a geographical region where the manifestation of God's presence is powerfully evident characterizes all great revivals.

God's awesome manifest presence in the Hebrides was accompanied by a deep consciousness of God's holiness that resulted in a solemn fear of God and deep conviction of sin among believers and unbelievers alike. Once the revival began at Barvas, people came from all four corners of the island on 14 busses, crowding the church to overflowing. Seven men were being driven to the meeting in a butcher's truck, when suddenly the Spirit of God fell on them. In great conviction all were converted before they reached the church.[6]

Another example of atmosphere change occurred when the above-mentioned revival service was concluding. A messenger arrived with an urgent request for the preacher:

> Come with me. There's a crowd of people outside the police station; they are weeping and in awful distress. We don't know what's wrong with them; but they are calling for someone to come and pray for them.[7]

While making his way to the police station, the preacher saw scenes that he never thought would be possible.

> Under a starlit sky, men and women were kneeling everywhere, by the roadside, outside the cottages, even behind the peat stacks, crying for God to have mercy upon them! Nearly 600 people, who had been making their way to the church, when suddenly the Spirit of God had fallen upon them in great conviction—like Paul on the way to Damascus causing them to fall to their knees in repentance![8]

This is an outstanding feature of every outpouring of the Holy Spirit. Seventy-five percent of those saved in the Hebrides Revival were saved outside of church buildings. The atmospheric change that comes with open manifestation of God's presence causes people to cry out like Isaiah wherever they are.

> *Woe is me, for I am undone!*
> *Because I am a man of unclean lips,*
> *And I dwell in the midst of a people of unclean lips;*
> *For my eyes have seen the King,*
> *The LORD of hosts* (Isa. 6:5 NKJV).

In great revivals when the spiritual atmosphere changes and the oppressive darkness is broken, people suddenly see *the awesomeness of God* and *the awfulness of sin* with its horrendous costliness. Charles Finney (1792–1875) once observed that in order for sin to be forgiven, it cost God His only Son. If sin remains unforgiven, it costs the sinner his life and an eternity in hell. The eternal consequence of sin always comes back into clear focus during revival and spiritual awakening.

6. Revival is Controversial!

Great revivals are controversial periods of history because they are supernormal days, the unusual is happening. Skeptics of revival often attribute it as nothing more than psychological phenomena involving excessive emotionalism and mass hysteria that sometimes happens among uneducated and simple-minded people. However, revival is a work of God, not a product of man. It is true that genuine revival inevitably produces spiritual excitement and is accompanied by all kinds of manifestations that involve the emotions, but it has nothing to do with hysteria.

Some of the revival manifestations are strange and an offense to religious-minded people and to arrogant humanists. But God often offends the mind in order to reveal the true condition of the heart. Anywhere there is human life, there is going to be human emotion; if there is no emotion, there is probably no life. Moreover, all kinds of people participate in revival when it comes: educated and uneducated, emotional and phlegmatic, rich and poor, and people in every part of the world, with every kind of temperament and every imaginable ethnic and socio-economic background.

Great revival is controversial for the same reason that God in the flesh was controversial. Jesus said that which men esteem is detestable in God's sight; and that which God esteems is despised by men. God's ways are higher than man's ways and are generally not understood or received by men.

The Church of England expelled George Whitefield (1714–1770) and John Wesley because of revival fire in their preaching and because of the manifestations of the Spirit in their services. All great revivals have been controversial in the eyes of religion and the worldly-minded. If we do not *know* God intimately and *understand* His ways, we will likely be offended in the days of His visitation. This pattern is everywhere present in classic revival history.

7. Revival is Contagious!

Great revival is fresh fire from heaven. Wherever it occurs, it spreads with amazing rapidity before the winds of the Spirit, just as fire in the natural spreads quickly over a dry prairie when driven by the wind.

Authentic revival seldom is confined to one congregation, though it may begin in a local church or a single geographical location. Revival pervades the atmosphere like a holy contagion and bursts out in unexpected places *as if carried by unseen hands*. Great revival can sweep over an entire city or region quickly and then spread to a larger district, state, nation, or nations with momentous results. An example of the contagious nature of revival is the Moravian Revival that occurred at Herrnhut in Germany on August 13, 1727, and then spread to different parts of Europe and England (1730s), to America (1730s), and to other locations abroad.

In our twentieth century world, because of rapid international travel, satellite communication systems and the internet, our world—for better or worse—is now a global community. Great revival fire can conceivably burn simultaneously all over the world as a unique end-time revival phenomenon unprecedented in history, until the knowledge of God and evidence of His glory literally cover the earth as the waters cover the sea.

Ponder this possibility in light of Isaiah's prophetic cry:

> *Oh, that you would rend the heavens and come down, that the mountains would tremble before you!* [2]*As when fire sets twigs ablaze and causes water to boil, come down to make your name known to your enemies and cause the nations to quake before you!"* (Isa. 64:1–2). *Then the nations clearly, "will see the glory of the LORD, the splendor of our God* (Is. 35:2).

8. Revival Is Marked by Multitudes Being Saved!

If the presence of the living God is glorious and awesome, His presence is also fearful. When the presence and holiness of God is manifest in a community, the fear of the Lord pervades the community at every level. His manifest presence brings people from every walk of life to a place where they are God-conscious and actually fear God regardless of previous biases or worldview. But without the manifest presence of God, there will be no fear of God in society or the church. We need to encounter Him before we can fear Him.

When there is awareness of God's manifest presence and the light of His holiness, this always reveals man's own sinfulness and need for cleansing (Isa. 6:5). Isaiah's encounter with the manifest presence of God in Isaiah 6 was dramatic. The posts of the door were shaken by the voice of the angel announcing God's holiness and glory. The house was filled with smoke (the shekinah glory).

Isaiah responded by crying out: "Woe is me, for I am undone! Because I am a man of unclean lips. *And I dwell in the midst of a people of unclean lips.*" How did Isaiah know his lips and those of his people were unclean? Isaiah gives the answer when he said: "For my eyes have seen the King, the LORD of hosts" (Isa. 6:5, NKJV).

During a revival from heaven, salvation spreads rapidly like a great spiritual epidemic. In the American Revival of

1857–58 that erupted in New York City and spread through the nation, sinners standing at the bars, gamblers at game tables, people gathered in churches, and even passengers and sailors on ships approaching the New York harbor, found themselves suddenly aware of God's presence and holiness. Overcome with their consciousness of God and smitten by the sudden awareness of their own sinfulness, they repented of their sins and turned to God in large numbers.

When spiritual awakening happens in a community or region, typically great numbers of sinners are saved in a short span of time. It is spiritual harvest time! The church must be ready to send forth laborers for the harvest. Evangelism is at its peak of effectiveness during days of a revival from heaven.

The multitudes being saved during great revival also must be discipled to Jesus and taught the Word of God so that their minds can be transformed concerning the character of God, a biblical worldview, the kingdom of God and allegiance to the Lord Jesus Christ, the message of the gospel, and how to spiritually reproduce in the power of the Spirit.

9. Revival Produces Enduring Fruit

Great revivals are a time of great fruitfulness. "God's presence and power are so mightily and extensively at work during revival that God accomplishes more in hours or days than usually results from years of faithful nonrevival ministry. . . . Many prayers that have gone unanswered for years are gloriously answered."[8]

Historically, revival converts are **quality fruit** that usually lasts over time. Revival converts tend to be lasting converts because they "have a permanent reverential awe of God and an abiding love for Christ. They have a deeper understanding and appreciation of the grace of God."[9]

Revival converts are more like New Testament conversions

where sinners are lavishly forgiven, the power of sin decisively broken, the demons of hell are cast out, their strongholds are shattered, and a clear-cut separation from the spirit of the age occurs.

Revival converts are born in fire, they carry fire, they spread fire and they are always hungry for more! Their conversion is much more like the powerful New Testament conversions and less like the mediocre conversions that characterize the compromised and lukewarm church in Western world nations. When the Bible talks about the great falling away at the end of the age, falling away will not be revival converts but the lukewarm "convinced" believers in church pews who are still tied to the world.

The **quantity** of revival fruit is somewhat linked to the duration of revival. If the second phase (visitation) and third phase (transformation) of revival continue for twenty years or more, obviously the quantity of fruit (all things being equal) will be greater than if the revival lasts only two years. This also relates to the **quality** of revival fruit that remains and to the effectiveness with which the revival baton is placed in the hands of the next generation.

10. Revival Is Preceded by Extraordinary Prayer

God always uses the corporate intercessory prayers of a humble people as His appointed means for cutting a channel from heaven to earth whereby He pours out His Spirit in revival for the church and in spiritual awakening for the world. As Matthew Henry (1662–1714) once remarked, "When God intends great mercy for His people, the first thing He does is to set them a-praying."

J. Edwin Orr, in a video titled "The Role of Prayer and Spiritual Awakening," asks this question: "Does prayer make revival happen?" He answers the question, "No! But it does make revival possible." Heart-rending prayer for revival encompasses other things like enormous longing for God, desperation, bro-kenness, repentance, humility, and faith. But the one over-arch-ing reality among God's people when preparing for revival is always persevering, passionate, pleading prayer.[10]

Edwin Orr concludes in his video, "God has chosen to limit Himself in relation to revival to the prayer of His people. Whether you are a Calvinist or an Arminian, the answer is the same: 'We must pray! No prayer, no revival!'"[11]

Extraordinary revival is preceded by extraordinary prayer! God partners with desperate believers who are willing "to pre-pare the way for the Lord" and His visitation. There is much evidence that God plans His own visits to those places where the preparation includes deep humility, focused prayer, and a persevering longing for Him to come.

Wesley L. Duewel believes that the deeper the hunger and the more widespread the intercession of the saints, the more broad scaled the spiritual awakening is likely to be. He adds, "There is usually a price of prayer to be paid in revival, and some people somewhere pay it."[12]

11. Revival Is Accompanied by Prophetic Preaching

By prophetic preaching we do not mean prophesying nor preaching about biblical prophecy or future events, though revival preaching usually does recapture the New Testament message and urgency of Jesus' second coming. By prophetic preaching we mean the kind of preaching that Peter did on the Day of Pentecost when the Holy Spirit descended from heaven's throne room. It is preaching empowered by the Holy Spirit, inspired by the Spirit of truth and revelation, and anointed by the Spirit with unction and urgency.

Prophetic preaching is Spirit-filled preaching. The Holy Spirit convicts and convinces of sin, the need of righteousness and of judgment to come. Revival preaching has in it the Spirit's anointing that motivates the unsaved hearer to respond, "What must we do to be saved?" The crowds at Pentecost were drawn by the magnetism of the Spirit and then exposed to this kind of Spirit-inspired preaching by Peter.

Prophetic revival preaching is like a sharp arrow that hits the mark with impact. It is preaching that has a prophetic edge, immediately relevant to the hearers, pierces the conscience, and moves those who are convicted of sin to respond to God's mercy. This kind of preaching is well illustrated by Charles Finney's description of a town in New York when revival broke out.

> The Spirit of God came upon me with such power, that it [preaching] was like opening a battery [of artillery] upon them [the people present]. For more than an hour, and perhaps for an hour and a half, the word of God came through me to them in a manner that I could see was carrying all before it. It was [as] a fire and a hammer breaking the rock; and as the sword that was piercing. . . . I saw that a general conviction was spreading over the whole congregation.[13]

Arthur Wallis observes that "the one simple explanation of the effects of revival preaching is the power of the Holy Spirit resting upon the preacher. Peter had been newly filled. His preaching was the overflow. A man may not possess great gifts of eloquence, but if he has this anointing his ministry will be effective."[14]

12. Revival Restores Lost Biblical Truth

In God's wisdom, the purpose of every great revival extends wider than the conversion of sinners. Among the numerous purposes of God in historic revivals is the restoration of some important truth or reality of God that has been lost. Revival is a catalyst to advance the church from its present state to the next level of restoration on the road to the full manifestation of God's glory in the earth.

Revival always brings a new infusion of spiritual life and power to the church! But great revival either sows the seed for recovery or fully restores to God's church some essential biblical truth or living reality of God that Satan in previous history has stolen from the church. Thus, the history of revival is the history of restoring biblical truth and revelation, spiritual understanding and reality, and renewed life to the church of Jesus Christ.

In classic revival history (AD 1500 to the present), God has been *progressively* restoring to the church what was progressively lost, hidden, or stolen from the church during the previous 1400 years of church history. During the Protestant Reformation (1517–1648), for example, God restored to the church biblical authority, justification by faith and the priesthood of all believers—basic biblical truths that had been lost to mainstream Christianity. The next great revival era restored an evangelical understanding of conversion and the true calling and mission of the church. God's progressive purpose and activity in each successive revival era has and will play an important role in restoring God's church to the fullness of her destiny in Christ.[13]

In summary, the return of God's manifest presence in revival lays a biblical, spiritual, and experiential foundation for the knowledge of God to be fully realized as *living truth* before Christ Jesus returns for His bride.

Understanding the significance of God's awesome "deeds" in classic revivals impacts our hearts, enlarges our vision and helps us understand what God is presently doing. It also imparts faith, and gives the Holy Spirit greater access to our hearts to stir within us deep desire and earnest intercession for even greater things happening today. In order to persevere as revival intercessors, we must know God Himself and understand His "ways" concerning revival. God instructs us in

Scripture to remember or reflect on His previous mighty acts of redemption as part of His preparation for using the present generation.

With Habakkuk let's pray—*LORD, I have heard of your fame; I stand in awe of your deeds, O LORD. Renew them in our day, in our time make them known* (Hab. 3:2).

4

Societal Impact of Great Revivals

They will rebuild the ancient ruins and restore the places long
devastated; they will renew the ruined cities that have been
devastated for generations (Isaiah 64:1)

G reat revivals have a supernatural and transformational
impact not only on individual lives, but also on entire
families, congregations, and even on the whole of society itself. In the wake of the catalytic influence of a great revival,
revival history testifies that the various spheres of society can
be redemptively impacted and changed by the manifest presence and power of God.

Numerous times in classic revivals, God has not only revived the church but also impacted society. When the heavens are opened and God pours out His Spirit, a change in the
spiritual atmosphere happens in a community or region that
makes possible the transformation of society.

God does not intend for revival to end with the church!
Neither does God intend for revival to end with evangelism.
Evangelism is not the ultimate goal; God never asked us to
make converts but disciples. Being born again is just the beginning! After rebirth, believers must grow and develop into
their new life in Christ through sanctification, transformation
and redemption in all its dimensions. This process of growing
and developing toward maturity in Christ applies both to the

individual and to the corporate body of Christ. Revived believers whose minds have been renewed according to biblical and kingdom values can become agents of revival, hope, and transformational healing in society.

Corporately, revived believers who carry revival fire and who have been transformed by the renewing of their mind carry the necessary light and anointing to introduce change and transformation in their community. Disciples of Jesus Christ who live and work in society become salt and light as agents of change in society

God intends for the manifestation of His presence and power to affect the society in which revival occurs. When spiritual breakthrough occurs, spiritual leaders must champion the things that attract God's presence—unity, prayer, humility, and holiness—and redemptive societal changes will begin to happen.

Classic revivals have historically elevated the moral conscience of the church and raised the moral level of the society in which they have occurred. As a consequence of the moral and spiritual awakening that comes with a great revival, righteous changes are introduced to the marketplace, social reforms are set in motion, which in turn restores justice and compassion for the poor and oppressed in society. In summary, great revivals will have transformational impact on society as the following examples reveal.

Eighteenth Century English Revival

The eighteenth century Evangelical Awakening in England (1730–1740) was not just about "saving souls" but also about societal transformation. This century of historic revival in John Wesley's day resulted in reformation that made society more just and more in harmony with the righteousness of God.

Historians and popular writers have described eighteenth

century England's social condition as being exceedingly ugly and "black with every kind of wickedness." The church had been reduced to impotent tradition. Most clergy were without faith. One could hardly find members in the House of Commons who attended church. Schools were reserved for the elite and wealthy. Some segments of the nation prospered financially but the common people were generally locked into poverty, ignorance and brutality.[1]

Prisons were overcrowded and the squalor of open sewers ran through prison cells as well as through the street ditches of city neighborhoods. Vast numbers of people died from diseases as a result of these open sewers. The theatre plays and novels of the day contributed to the deplorable moral decay. Mob violence was common in the over-crowded cities. "Infant mortality was appallingly high," as 74.5% of the infants died before age five. Alcohol consumption had increased tenfold in 40 years.[2]

But God countered England's spiritual, moral, and social devastation with a revival that eventually impacted the entire nation through the preaching of reformists such as:

- George Whitefield
- John Wesley
- Charles Wesley
- thousands of lay Methodist preachers
- the Puritans
- anti-slavery movement led by reformers like John Newton (author of "Amazing Grace"), and
- William Wilberforce

During this English century the poor heard the gospel gladly, multitudes of lives were transformed, prison reform began, poverty and alcoholism were greatly reduced, and working conditions of the poor improved. Wilberforce and other dedicated Christian leaders led the way in seeing Parliament pass moral and social reforms in various areas such as homes for refugee slaves and the starting of Bible track and mission societies. Parliament also agreed to allow missionaries to go to India and chaplains were provided for the East India Company employees. In 1807, as an overflow of the revival in the 1700s, Parliament abolished the slave trade. A few years later Parliament passed the emancipation of all British slaves. [3]

The historian Élie Halévy's (1870–1937) famous thesis is that England was spared the social revolutions that convulsed Europe from 1789 onwards. He believes that England was spared primarily because the English eighteenth century revival so transformed the English spirit and social landscape that the nation therefore shrunk from socio-political revolution.

Nineteenth Century American Revivals

J. Edwin Orr calls the Laymen's Prayer Revival of 1857–1859 the "greatest event" of the nineteeth century. This spiritual tornado that began in New York City and the Northeast became the focal point of an enormous awakening as the Spirit of God swept through the nation. In some towns it was reported as being "almost impossible" to find an adult who had not been converted. [4]

In many American towns and cities bars, theaters, and gambling houses closed or emptied, new churches sprang up, and family altars of prayer were established or restored. The spirit of prayer grew in intensity until anyone crossing the land could find a "mid-day" prayer meeting in almost any town. As many as 50,000 people a week encountered Jesus and salvation when this gracious visitation was at its height. Many who were saved became preachers and pioneer missionaries who were commissioned to go with the gospel to the ends of the earth. [5]

Other nineteenth century revivals in America resulted in a variety of moral and social reforms. Church and civic leaders impacted by the revivals led the way in condemning slavery as an extraordinary sin that infected every aspect of life, thus birthing the abolitionist movement. The temperance movement was also birthed and effected the banning of alcohol in thirteen northern states. Other societal transformation included urban reforms that helped rid city governments of corruption and passed laws protecting children by providing all children education and setting strict limits on child labor. Nineteenth century revivals also contributed to the emergence of the women's suffrage movement.

Timothy Smith, in an award-winning book, *Revivalism and Social Reform,*[6] documents clearly how nineteenth century revivals—like Charles G. Finney, the Frontier Camp Meetings (1805–1840), the Laymen's Prayer Revival that started in New York City, and the Holiness Movement—all had widespread transforming social impact upon the fabric of the nation and on the abolition of slavery before and after the Civil War.[7] Even secular historians heralded Smith's book when it appeared as providing clear evidence that the strongest voices against slavery in the nations were those impacted by great revival awakenings!

Salvation Army Revival

William (1829–1912) and Catherine (1829–1890) Booth (English Methodists) were God's nineteenth century champions for the poor—first in England and then all over the world. This extraordinary husband-wife team brought revival to the smelly "sin slums" of London's East End. They both lived their lives entirely for God and the poor, not for themselves, as they targeted sin, poverty, and social injustice.

This revolutionary couple birthed one of the most amazing revival ministries on the earth.[8] Their battle cry was "Go for souls, and go for the worst!" Their banner was "Blood and Fire." On behalf of the poor in London's worst slums, William Booth and his disciples relentlessly went to the dangerous streets as "salvation warriors"—often returning bleeding and battered, clothes torn, and band instruments smashed. The police did little to protect or assist them. Catherine wrote that William would stumble home night after night wounded and "haggard with fatigue."

Catherine inspired many of the Salvation Army's organizational and social policies. William's fiery sermons drove the gospel message home. Converts became numerous and willing to leave their past behind and start a new life as a soldier in "The Salvation Army."[9] The "Army" reached multitudes ignored by London's churches! The Booths began a revolutionary revival magazine called *War Cry* in 1879.

Catherine's campaign against child prostitution resulted in the legal age of consent in England being raised from 13 to 16 years-of-age. When Catherine was weak and dying of cancer, she exhorted her husband to develop plans for clearing the Victorian slums of London.[10] In response, William wrote his book, *In Darkest England—and the Way Out*. It became a best seller and a firestorm of controversy, addressing the redemptive solution to England's poverty and vice.

When William Booth died in 1912, 150,000 people in London filed past his coffin and 40,000 attended his funeral that included Queen Mary of England, who sat next to an ex-prostitute and convert of General Booth. The "Army" at Booth's death was having a transforming impact in 58 countries and 34 languages![11] Today the Salvation Army is in 102 countries worldwide. Only eternity will reveal the vast redemptive impact of the Booths and the Salvation Army.

Welsh Revival of 1904

October 1904 stands out in the little nation of Wales as a month and year never to be forgotten. The Spirit of God swept across Wales until mountains and valleys, cities and villages were filled with open manifestations of God's presence. Churches, previously sparsely attended, became crowded and meetings went on day and night. Prayer, singing, and testimony could be heard in overflowing congregations in village after village throughout Wales.

At year's end (1904), "Wales was ablaze with God" (G. Campbell Morgan, 1863–1945). Twenty-thousand converts were recorded in five weeks and 100,000 converts in six months. As the powerful, manifest presence of God swept over hundreds of villages and cities—taverns, theaters and dance halls were emptied— the churches were filled night after night with praying multitudes. In the banks and stores, on the trains and in the schools—everywhere people were talking about God until almost every home in the nation felt its impact. Newspapers carried reports about the spiritual awakening.

God's kingdom was becoming radically invasive and pervasive, impacting redemptively entire communities. One observer reported that the courts and jails were deserted and the police found themselves without work to do.

One account reports about "policemen who closed their station and formed a choir to sing at the revival meetings. Long-standing debts were repaid, church and family feuds were healed and a new unity of purpose was felt across the denominational divides."[12]

> So great was the fear of God and conviction of sin that gripped the people, that in some communities crime disappeared—judges were presented with a blank paper, as no cases waited to be tried. And to commemorate the occasion, they were presented with white gloves. In more

than one place the post office's supply of money order blanks were exhausted as people sought to make restitution by paying their debts!

Bars and theaters closed while stores were sold out of Bibles and Testaments. Members of parliament, who were busy attending revival services, postponed their political meetings; theatrical companies coming into districts found no audiences, for "all the world was praying." Temperance workers saw the Spirit of God accomplish more in three months than they had accomplished in forty years.[13]

Twentieth Century Brazilian Revival

The Holy Spirit has moved mightily in Brazil since 1910–1915 when a few Western missionaries carried revival fire from the Welsh and Azusa Street Revivals to that nation. Three great waves of Pentecostal revival subsequently occurred in Brazil during the twentieth century: 1910–1930; 1950–1970; 1970s–1990s.

As a result of Brazil's century-long revival, eight-in-ten Protestants in Brazil became either Pentecostal or charismatic. Roughly half of Brazilian Catholics became charismatic according to a 2006 survey.[14]

As the revival in eighteenth century England had extensive transforming impact on society, similar dynamics have occurred in twentieth century Brazil. There was a steady upward move in Brazil among the urban poor because of revival. Pentecostal churches subsequently appeared in almost all of the nation's poor neighborhoods. Salvation resulted in a ground swell of wholesome social change at almost every level of society.

Revival converts in Brazil departed from the path of self-perpetuating poverty and embraced a redemptive lifestyle. Converts were delivered from destructive behavior associated with alcohol, smoking, gambling, immoral sex, pornography, violence, and drugs. Consequently, for them domestic violence ceased, family values were adopted, honesty and a good work ethic was developed, spendable income among the poor increased, and the people understood these blessings were from God.

Health problems among the poor—a persistent crisis in Brazil's health services—were impacted by the Pentecostal revival with its emphasis on physical healing and deliverance. One writer called the revival a "health delivery system."[15]

The revival provided Brazil's lower class with a strong sense of community and belonging, dignity and value expressed even in their physical appearance. Revival worship services met the deep longing of the heart for God's presence, for beauty, for joy, and for celebration. They worshipped God with abandonment for having delivered them from their cycle of sin and poverty, and for having put their life and families back together again.

Forbes magazine, in an excellent article (1990), assessed the revival and vibrantly growing Pentecostal movement in Brazil and believed it was laying "the cultural foundations"[16] for significant transformational change in the nation socially, economically and politically. Gilberto, a leader of the Brazilian Assemblies of God, believes the spread of the Gospel in Brazil "holds the promise of transforming his society. . . ."[17]

The Hebrides Revival

The Hebrides Revival (1949–1953) stands out in the twentieth century as a revival with societal impact. The Hebrides islands (just off the Atlantic coast of Scotland) had a revival that some have referred to as the last undisputable revival that included *community transformation* in the Western world (until 2010). This revival interestingly embodies four important features that we are now seeing widespread in non-Western nations in the twenty-first century where there is transforming revival.

The revival erupted when the Hebrides' pastor at Barvas and his seven elders took seriously God's covenant promise in 2 Chronicles 7:13–15, believing it applied not only to Solomon's generation, but also to the blood-washed covenant believers in their generation. They heard God speaking to them in these words—*When I shut up heaven . . . , if My people who are called by My name will humble themselves, and pray and seek My face, and turn from their wicked ways, then I will hear from heaven. . . .* (2 Chron. 7:13–14, NKJV).

They appealed to God, according to His instruction in this passage as a covenant-keeping God, who keeps His covenant promises and faithfully fulfills His Word. As they humbly submitted to God's authority in this Scripture, they made their requests known to Him with faith in the integrity of His Word and His faithfulness to do what He promised. They believed if they did their part, God would do His part. They did their part with the humility of a lamb and the boldness of a lion that only the blood of Jesus makes possible. Consequently they were heard in the throne room of heaven and the rain of the Spirit fell on their islands.[18] It is no coincidence that all contemporary transformed communities also have followed God's instruction in 2 Chronicles 7:14–15 as part of their intentional preparation for the coming of God's manifest presence.

When describing the initial breakthrough in the Hebrides Revival, eyewitnesses testified that the presence and power of God began to sweep down on the island of Lewis. Duncan Campbell's words were: "Revival had come and the power that was let loose in that barn shook the whole . . . of Lewis."[19] Campbell also said that the community of Barvas (the hot center of the revival) was "a community saturated with God."[20]

The presence of God was in fact everywhere in the communities, not just in the churches—even at the places of entertainment and schools. First-hand witnesses of the revival testified that there was a general public awareness of God's holy presence over the islands. It was initially strongest on the Isle of Lewis; then it spread to the other islands. Prayers were quickly heard and answered by God with measurable results in people's lives and society at all levels.

The revival was strongly presence-based. Because the heavens over the Hebrides were open, there was a deep and immediate consciousness of God's presence everywhere. This resulted in a solemn fear of God in the marketplaces, homes, and public places accompanied by acute conviction of sin in believers and unbelievers alike. People everywhere were getting saved.

During the revival, in spite of the churches being filled to overflowing with multiple services each night and people getting saved, seventy-five percent of all people who were converted during the revival were saved outside the church. Because God's manifest presence was everywhere, there was an explosion of salvation. The Bible and history reveal that God's manifest presence is required to affect a real, tangible, and redemptive change in society.

There was both an immediate and long-lasting transformational impact on society. Sufficient numbers of people's lives on the islands were dramatically changed by their encounter with God that the social landscape changed dramatically for the better in community after community. Their municipalities, homes, churches, and social structures were all impacted by the revival.

During the revival, marriages were healed, families were restored, and drinking houses were closed. Societal changes occurred at the community and township level in relation to youth, education, and business. Long-term change occurred in the youth as they became zealous disciples of Jesus Christ. Many youth who before were bored and uninterested in God or church, as revival converts they became pastors, church leaders, and life-long missionaries. God's presence and love impacted young and old alike at every level of the communities.

In summary, these six accounts of historic revivals in the eighteenth, nineteenth, and twentieth centuries illustrate clearly that during times of great revival, God impacts communities and society broadly in a harvest way (salvation) and in a kingdom way (transformation). God is presently doing it again in the twenty-first century in unlikely places like Guatemala, Columbia, Uganda, Fiji, Papua New Guinea, Canadian Arctic, and Kentucky.

5

Spiritual Revolutionaries and Great Revivals

As servants of God we commend ourselves in every way:
. . .in truthful speech and in the power of God;
with weapons of righteousness in the right hand
and in the left; . . . genuine, yet regarded as
impostors; . . .beaten, and yet not killed;
. . . having nothing, and yet possessing everything

(2 Corinthians 6:4–10

Great revivals have always been led by leaders who were kingdom visionaries and spiritual revolutionaries. They carried God's fire and were able to communicate His heart clearly to others in their generation. They were individuals who paid a high price personally to partner with God for revival, restoration, and transformation of the church. They summed up in themselves, in an intense form, the very thing God was longing to restore to His church in the new generation. Like John the Baptist, they were men or women sent from God on a specific mission and with a specific message.

The gospel is essentially a revolutionary message that is best proclaimed by those who share the revolutionary Spirit of Jesus. Then and now, spiritual revolutionaries are humble vessels who develop a history of intimacy with God and who champion those things which attract God's presence

and anointing. Like Jesus' disciples, who had a revolutionary spirit and "turned Jerusalem upside down," spiritual
revolutionaries carry God's spiritual DNA for the new thing
He is doing or about to do in the world. As a result, they
become catalytic agents for advancing Jesus' kingdom on
the earth and for moving the church forward into the next
generation.

Revolutionaries have an unshakable faith in God, an overwhelming sense of a divine calling to serve God in their generation, an empowering by the Holy Spirit to move mountains of impossibility, and a firm determination to fulfill their
destiny, even if it's at the expense of life itself! They have a
strong awareness of God's holiness and an uncompromising
conviction about God and the message they carry from Him.
Like Elijah who was a "troubler" in Israel, they disturb and often offend the church in its status quo condition and therefore
tend to be controversial figures. They are men or women of
clear prophetic vision and uncompromising moral integrity.

They are individuals who have eaten the scroll! Subsequently, the Word of God in them is like a hammer, like a fire,
and like a sharp double-edged sword. They are messengers
who challenge the social and moral conscience of the church.
They cannot tolerate lukewarm Christianity, injustice, or pre-
tense! Though they may not carry the whole council of God,
their message is nonetheless vital for change and revival in
their generation! Through them the voice of the Lord is heard.
They are neither an "echo" nor one of the clamoring voices in
church circles. Instead they speak with authority, a message
that communicates clearly God's heart and His present word
for the church.

All spiritual revolutionaries are risk takers in their generation
for the sake of Christ. They intuitively know by the Spirit and
from the Scriptures that things are not right in the church and
that God wants them changed. Who will be the risk takers and

heroes of faith in this generation? There is a difference between reading about history and making history! Somebody has to venture out in faith into uncharted waters in each generation before there can be a historic revival.

Those most willing to risk and venture are normally those who have the least invested in the status quo, who are most spiritually hungry, most courageous, and most willing to live counter to the present religious system, to humanistic values, to self-centered living, and who most desire spiritual reformation and transformation.

A spiritual "revolution" involves radical change for the sake of a fresh kingdom expression of God's justice and righteousness on the earth. God's revolutionary kingdom provides liberation for the captive, justice for the poor, equality for gender and ethnic groups, wisdom and integrity in government and transformation for communities, nations and the land.

It's important to understand that in God's kingdom we are not *starting* a revolution, we are *joining* a revolutionary King in His revolution. When we choose His kingdom, by definition we choose a revolution from the status quo. If, however, we choose to remain in the status quo, we remain under the influence of the spirit of the age and we forfeit His kingdom.

Old Testament Revolutionaries

The spiritual giants in the Old Testament are too numerous to mention and they were all spiritual revolutionaries in their generation. Hebrews 11 lists some of these great men and women of faith in the Old Testament, the foremost of which is Abraham.

Abraham

Abraham, the father of the Jewish people, started a revolution of covenant faith in *Yahweh*. God asked him to leave his wealthy lifestyle and home in a protected, walled city to go on a pilgrimage of faith and to wait for God's promise for many years in the midst of much adversity. In hope against hope, he trusted God and believed the promise until it became his inheritance. Abraham took a great risk in order to fulfill God's destiny for his life and birth the covenant people of faith.

Moses

Moses, the founder of Israel as a nation, was a revolutionary leader whom God appointed to lead the Jewish people out of Egyptian slavery. Moses dealt with the tremendous tension between present adversity and future promise by a God whom he could not see. He fully gave his life for the unseen future and the impossible dream.

Other Old Testament Spiritual Revolutionaries

Hebrews records that Old Testament revolutionaries like Joshua, Gideon, Deborah, David, Samuel, and prophets like Elijah and Daniel *"through faith" conquered kingdoms, administered justice, and gained what was promised; who shut the mouths of lions, quenched the fury of the flames, and escaped the edge of the sword; whose weakness was turned to strength; and who became powerful in battle and routed foreign armies* (Heb. 11:33–34).

Still other unnamed and heroic Old Testament revolutionaries

> *. . . were tortured and refused to be released, so that they might gain a better resurrection. Some faced jeers and flogging, while still others were chained and put in prison. They were stoned; they were sawed in two; they were put to death by the sword. They went about in sheepskins and goatskins, destitute, persecuted and mistreated the world was not worthy of them. [For the sake of God's revolutionary kingdom] they wandered in deserts and mountains, and in caves and holes in the ground* (Heb. 11:35–38).

New Testament Revolutionaries

The New Testament begins with the Jews living again in Israel, but under the oppressive rule of the Romans. Simultaneously, it begins with the revolutionary ministry of John the Baptist, reminiscent of the Elijah of old.

John the Baptist

John confronted directly, not the Roman government, but the clergy and religious status quo of his day. The revolutionary character of his ministry is seen in the response of the religious leaders who had not authorized John's ministry and in the unprecedented baptizing of Jews! Both issues were unthinkable by the status quo! John declared that if they thought his baptizing with water was revolutionary, the greater Spirit-baptism of the Messiah would be even more so (John 1:26–27), baptizing "with the Holy Spirit and with fire" (Matt. 3:11; Luke 3:16).

John further disturbed the religious status quo by calling Jesus *"the Lamb of God who takes away the sin of the world"* (John 1:29b). In so doing, John was prophetically proclaiming the cross even before Jesus began His public ministry as did Isaiah (Isa. 53:7). The Temple lambs were sacrifices for Israel; Jesus is God's Lamb that is sacrificed for the whole world.

John's preaching was that of a prophetic voice being heard in Israel again after 400 years of silence. His voice was strong, confrontative, fearless, and convicting. John's revolutionary message called for thorough repentance of sin at every level of society and religion. As many as half of Jesus' twelve disciples were part of John the Baptist's revival before they joined Jesus.

Jesus of Nazareth

The earthly ministry of Jesus Christ was truly revolutionary! As His followers, we are not called to join a leaderless revolution; we are called to follow a revolutionary King! When Jesus came in the incarnation, He introduced a kingdom that is not of this world and He came to open the door to that kingdom to all those who would follow Him. Jesus is the history maker extraordinaire! He came as a great "disturber" of the religious status quo! He is the foremost kingdom revolutionary and the most radical message ever proclaimed in history!

The revolutionary nature of Jesus' mission is evident in the cleansing of the Jerusalem Temple (overthrowing the tables of the money changers, scattering their coins), the challenging of the Pharisees with their religious tradition, and the introduction of a kingdom where the least becomes the greatest and the meek inherit the earth! Jesus clearly did not die on the cross to preserve the religious status quo! Neither did He die to pacify captivity to culture and the spirit of the age. Jesus came to confront everything Satan had defiled and sin had corrupted and to deliver His people who were caught in the yoke of the status quo. He took off the yokes of religion and Satan, and all other strongholds and mindsets that keep people in bondage.

Unlike other Jewish Rabbi's, Jesus did not teach a system of doctrine. He Himself was the message and He spoke in the language of life. His Sermon on the Mount is a revolutionary manifesto about the kingdom of God. The upside-down kingdom value system of the Sermon on the Mount is truly a revolutionary message that offends the natural mind.

Jesus and His disciples were essentially peace-loving, meek people, but they stirred-up the spiritual ream of darkness resulting in a collision course. Jesus, the spiritual revolutionary, is also the Prince of Peace. He is the Lion of the Tribe of Judah— bold and fearsome; but He is also the Lamb of God— meek and submissive to the Father. He identified His Messianic mission not with the sword, but with suffering— i.e., as the Suffering Servant of Isaiah 53 and with the cross. There's never been a revolutionary leader like the man Christ Jesus!

Twelve Apostles

The revolutionary strategy of Jesus is apparent in the selection of His twelve disciples. Instead of selecting gifted leaders from the religious system, He chose twelve men from outside the established religious system—men with passion and zeal for life. He spent His three years of public ministry mentoring these young leaders of the future.

The twelve were the first forerunners. Forerunners are the friends of the Bridegroom. They took on His nature, proclaimed His message, and advanced His kingdom that was not of this world. They prayed regularly and often as did Jesus, healed the sick and delivered people from demons and darkness—all in the same supernatural power of the Holy Spirit as did Jesus!

Other Disciples

Jesus trained a total of 72 disciples for ministry alongside the 12 before His death (c.f. Luke 10). After His death and resurrection, Jesus poured out His Spirit on 120 disciples who were giving themselves to prayer and waiting in obedience (Acts 1:14). When 3,000 Jews were converted on the Day of Pentecost, the 12, 72, 120, and the 3,000 became the nucleus for one of the most revolutionary communities and causes in all of history.

From the Four Gospels, we know that all these spiritual revolutionaries grew up in the status quo of their own generation. Familiarity with the status quo, however, rather than remaining entrapped, created the cry for deliverance in their hearts that became unstoppable. As believers, we will either be part of the revolution by advancing God's kingdom or by default find ourselves in opposition to Jesus by maintaining our allegiance to the status quo.

The Early Church

The 120 disciples of Jesus that gathered in the Upper Room prayer meeting until the Holy Spirit was poured out from heaven, were spiritual revolutionaries who carried the same spiritual "DNA" as their Lord. Having recovered from the chaos and trauma of Jesus' crucifixion, and filled with hope because of Jesus' resurrection, they waited in faith and obedience to Jesus' instruction until they were *"clothed with power from on high"* (Luke 24:49).

Judaism was the institutionalized religious status quo of the day. In contrast, the 12, the 120, along with the 3,000 Jews converted on the Day of Pentecost, became the core revolution that we now know of as "the early church."

The Book of Acts describes these committed Christians as a radical band that literally lived together as a community and ate their meals together. As a community, they were devoted to four values: the Apostles' teaching, *koinonia* fellowship, the breaking of bread, and prayer. Acts 2 further describes the early church community by saying—

> *Everyone was filled with awe, and many wonders and miraculous signs were done by the apostles. All the believers were together and had everything in common. Selling their possessions and goods, they gave to anyone as he had need. Every day they continued to meet together in the temple courts. They broke bread in their homes and ate together with glad and sincere hearts, praising God and enjoying the favor of all the people. And the Lord added to their number daily those who were being saved* (Acts 2:43—47).

This community of deeply committed believers was unmistakably filled with the Holy Spirit's presence, gifts, and power. Because they were characterized by the love of Christ, the fear of the Lord, unspeakable joy and generosity, and supernatural unity, *"the word of God spread. The number of disciples in Jerusalem increased rapidly, and a large number of* [Jewish] *priests became obedient to the faith"* (Acts 6:7).

The impact of this tiny minority, in the intimidating governmental system of the Roman Empire, was profound! Why? Because the church, in its beginning, was a revolutionary kingdom with a revolutionary spirit and led by a revolutionary leader who is *"the Living One"* that was dead but now alive forever, and who holds *"the keys of death and Hades"* (Rev. 1:18). This revolutionary company of committed disciples was disenfranchised, was free from the false security of mammon, and had no church buildings. But it did have the risen Lord and the fire of spiritual revolution burning as a bright flame. As a result the church rocked the entire Roman Empire for three centuries with profound transformational impact.

Apostle to the Gentiles

Paul's conversion, commissioning, and ministry among the Gentiles were all truly revolutionary—even in the eyes of the Jerusalem church. His strategy for carrying out the Gentile mission brought him into conflict with Jews all over the Roman world. Paul lived a life of self-denial, wrestling with the powers of darkness and demonstrating boldness in the face of hostile mobs. His continual praying and fasting, his tears, and travail for the churches were the expression of his own unquenchable passion for Jesus and burning desire that others might know Him also.

His life was one of single focus and undistracted devotion to his Lord. His own testimony was: *"I do all things for the sake of the gospel"* (1 Cor. 9:23). He said to believers at Philippi—*"for to me, to live is Christ and to die is gain"* (Phil. 1:21); *"whatever was to my profit I now consider loss for the sake of Christ"* (Phil. 3:7); *"I press on to take hold of that for which Christ Jesus took hold of me"* (Phil. 3:12); *"but one thing I do: Forgetting what is behind and straining toward what is ahead, I press on toward the goal . . ."*

(Phil. 3:13–14). Because of his revolutionary devotion to Christ Jesus, Paul died (like Peter) as a martyr in Rome at the hands of the evil emperor Nero.

Church History Revolutionaries

Because the church began with vibrant life and power but then declined into a corrupt institution during the "Dark Ages," Christian revolutionaries and revivalists were needed to bring the church to restoration and transformation.

As in biblical times, church history revolutionaries are gloriously too numerous to mention by name. God used Christian revolutionaries and revivalists to restore and transform the church. Even when the spiritual revolution was largely pushed underground during the "Dark Ages" (AD 500–1500), still the Lord Jesus found true revolutionaries to carry His light, and His word, and to be His voice. Since the Protestant Reformation (AD 1517), revolutionary spiritual leaders full of fire have been more prominent in the church again. Some of these we will mention by name, beginning with three pre-Reformation revolutionaries that helped make the Reformation possible.

John Wycliffe (ca. AD 1329–1384)

John Wycliffe—the "Morningstar of the Reformation"— was a distinguished student and teacher at Oxford. He fathered a spiritual revolution in fourteenth-century England. In Wycliffe's day, the Catholic Church dominated the nation spiritually and politically, with vast amounts of money from church taxation being sent to the Pope in Rome. Anyone who complained was threatened with excommunication and damnation. Spiritual superstition and biblical ignorance were rife in England. The people had no access to the Bible in their own language.

Like most spiritual revolutionaries, Wycliffe's conversion

was a blessed release from the oppression of lifeless religion, Satan, darkness, and death. He was soon faced with the reality that the church and its clergy bore no resemblance to Bible truths and the spiritual fire of the early church. He became the most powerful preacher in Great Britain and a radical reformer. Churches and lecture halls began to fill to hear him speak. People were stunned by his message as most churches were in Latin and had no preaching at all. As Wycliffe opened the Word of God and preached the gospel plainly in English, light and truth began to dawn!

With a revolutionary spirit like Jesus, Wycliffe confronted the unbiblical practices and doctrines of the church with dramatic impact on the population. He opposed the Catholic Church's oppression, translated the Bible into English and began a training center for lay preachers and evangelists.

He called his disciples "apostolic men" whom he commissioned to teach the people biblical truths unknown in England. These young revolutionaries, called Wycliffe's "Bible Men," wore simple brown cloaks with large pockets to carry and distribute portions of the Bible as they travelled from village to village preaching the Bible in the English language. The Spirit's anointing on them made them the most forceful speakers in the nation.

Soon a firestorm of persecution occurred. The church and its clergy were furious at these young zealots! But the church's resistance, however, did nothing to slow down this spiritual revolution that turned the nation upside down with the Word of God![1] When Wycliffe and his young preachers were driven underground, his revolution spread to Bohemia (Czech) where they impacted John Hus and paved the way for the Protestant Reformation that came some 150 years after Wycliffe's death.

John Hus (1369-1415)

John Hus was a fiery Bohemian (Czech) priest, reformer and forerunner of the Protestant Reformation, preceding Martin Luther by a century. Like John Wycliffe, John Hus emphasized the authority of Scripture over the authority of the church and pope.

Hus, a professor at the University at Prague, preached in the influential university church of Prague in the language of the people. This extraordinary preacher prophetically denounced many unbiblical practices in Roman Catholicism, and defined the Church by Christ-like living rather than by sacraments. His preaching caused the first tremors of the great spiritual earthquakes of the Reformation.

Because Hus refused to compromise the gospel, the Pope excommunicated him and ordered him burned at the stake outside the city of Prague as a heretic. Hus prophesied that his message of reform would be "a hidden seed" that would fall into the ground and die for a season, but would later sprout again to bear much fruit. This indeed happened 100 years later when the Protestant reformers picked up his message.

Girolamo Savonarola (1452-1498)

Girolamo Savonarola was a Dominican monk in Florence, Italy, whose righteous soul was provoked by all the sin and sexual immorality in the City of Florence. He became a spiritual revolutionary and the catalyst of a fiery revival in that famous city. At age 22, Savonarola wrote a paper entitled "Contempt of the World." In the paper he likened the sins of Florence to those of Sodom and Gomorrah. After studying the Scripture for years, waiting upon the Lord and devoted to prayer, God gave him a vision of coming judgment for the church. He began to preach with a prophetic voice to the people.

Revival fire broke out in power and gripped the whole

area. Savonarola's audience—men and women, poets and philosophers, craftsmen and laborers—all sobbed and wept for their sins. People walked the streets of Florence so gripped by conviction from the Holy Spirit that they were half-dazed and speechless.

Savonarola boldly preached even against papal immorality. After eight years of anointed, prophetic preaching in Florence as a spiritual revolutionary, Savonarola (not surprisingly) was tortured as a heretic, hanged to death, and his body burned in the city square. Afterward, his ashes were scattered by the jealous and angry priests. Savonarola became Martin Luther's spiritual hero and inspired him as the catalyst of another revolution called the Protestant Reformation.

Martin Luther (1483-1548)

Trained as a Roman Catholic monk and biblical scholar, Martin Luther started a spiritual revolution in Germany. With eyes enlightened by the Holy Spirit, he came to see that many of the church doctrines that he had been taught had no basis in Scripture. Luther subsequently believed that salvation was a new relationship to God totally based on God's Word and promises, not on human merit or works.

With this conviction burning like fresh fire in his bones, Luther nailed his 95 theses to a University door on October 31 1517. This was the equivalent of declaring spiritual war. He furthered the war with powerful tracts that set his generation on fire. Luther declared, "I have been born to war and fight with factions and devils."[2] The spiritual revolution that Luther ignited spread throughout Europe, and eventually the world, as the Protestant Reformation.

William Tyndale (1494–1536)

William Tyndale became a spiritual revolutionary in England when he defied the Roman Catholic Church by translating the New Testament into the contemporary English language of the people and publishing it in 1525. Tyndale, the biblical revolutionist, was condemned by the Roman Catholic Church as a heretic and burned at the stake on 6 October 1536. His last words were: "Lord, open the king of England's eyes."

Tyndale's final prayer was answered when Thomas Cranmer (1489–1556) and Thomas Cromwell (1485–1540) persuaded King Henry VIII to approve the publication of the Coverdale translation (heavily dependent upon Tyndale's translation). By 1539, every parish church in England was required to have a copy of the English Bible available to all of its parishioners, thus becoming the Bible of early Puritanism and the English Reformation. Being willing to lay down his life for the cause, Tyndale's legacy lives on.

About 90% of Tyndale's New Testament translated words also passed into the King James Version; about 75% into the English Revised Standard Version. Tyndale's revolutionary cause triumphed in the end!

Nikolaus Ludwig von Zinzendorf (1700–1760)

Nikolaus von Zinzendorf was greatly impacted by the revival of Pietism while a student in Germany. Coming from a wealthy European family, he inherited a large estate with acreage in eastern Germany (Moravia) and opened his estate as a place of refuge for persecuted Christians from Bohemia. Zinzendorf and the Bohemians (later known as the Moravians) built a village on his estate which they named Herrnhut, meaning "Watch of the Lord." Herrnhut became a peaceful revolutionary community characterized by simplicity and purity of devotion to Christ, faithful night and day prayer, and missionary vision and zeal in going to the nations.

Having been impacted by the revival of his day, Zinzendorf and the new community covenanted together to pray for revival. On August 13,1727, the Holy Spirit visited the Herrnhut community during a communion service. The revival that followed powerfully affected the entire community, young and old alike. As a result, 24 men and 24 women made a covenant together to pray in one-hour intercessory increments for the next 24 hours. The Moravians subsequently became a people of extraordinary prayer. The fire of God's presence so ignited the Herrnhut community that they gave themselves to an unbroken "watch of the Lord" in night and day prayer that continued for over 100 years!

The Moravians became known as a community sensitive to the Holy Spirit, radically devoted 24/7 night and day prayer, willing to sacrifice for the sake of the gospel, committed to sanctified unity, and the sending of missionaries to the nations with dedication and zeal unprecedented since the early church.

The spiritual revolution among the Moravian community resulted in one of the greatest missionary thrusts that the church has ever released on the earth! By 1795, *65 years* after unbroken prayer had begun, the small Moravian community had sent 300 missionaries to the ends of the earth!

The Moravians profoundly impacted John Wesley who later became a revolutionary leader himself in the great English revival. The Moravians' understanding of justification by faith and the freedom of the Holy Spirit, plus their radical commitment to prayer and the lost, greatly influenced Wesley's spiritual life and ministry.[3]

Church historians typically overlook the role of the Moravian community as the praying catalytic fire behind John Wesley and the Great Awakening in England and America.

John Wesley (1703-1791)

John Wesley and George Whitefield (1714–1770) were part of a revolutionary student organization at Oxford University called the "Holy Club." This was a group of students who were rigorously devoted to the spiritual disciplines of prayer, fasting, Bible study, the sacraments, visiting those in prison, ministering to the poor, and pursuing God together. When both Wesley and Whitefield entered into the assurance of salvation through faith in Christ alone, they began preaching the gospel with great anointing and impact. After becoming acquainted with the Moravians, they also devoted themselves to praying for revival.

Because of their anointed preaching and born-again message, Wesley and Whitefield began to be banned from preaching in the Anglican Church, even though both were ordained Anglican ministers. It was the revolutionary departure from tradition, first by Whitefield and then by Wesley, that led them to preach to coal miners in the fields near Bristol, England. This revolutionary initiative of preaching the gospel in the open fields actually became the occasion for the beginning of the Great Evangelical Revival/Awakening in eighteenth century England. Because they dared venture outside the church with the gospel, the revival spread rapidly.

Wesley went a step further than Whitefield in that he began to train and ordain lay preachers when the organized church would not consent to do so within its structure. Wesley and his lay preachers became fiery spiritual revolutionaries wherever they went preaching the gospel of salvation. Gripped by the revolutionary enterprise of Christ, Wesley gave up a teaching career at Oxford to preach the apostolic gospel to the poor. When he encountered resistance from the old structure of Anglicanism, his Spirit-led ministry created the new wineskin of Methodism through which the revival and its fruit continued for 100 years.

Wesley preached God's righteousness, coming judgment, and the forgiveness of sins to all who would listen in the fields and the streets of England. He preached with such Holy Spirit power that his words struck his listeners like a hammer and burned like fire. His preaching, full of biblical certainty and authority, brought great conviction to sinners and great assurance of faith to the converted.

As a true revolutionary leader, Wesley modeled simplicity and purity of devotion to Christ in his lifestyle, traveling, and preaching of the gospel. His lay preachers loved him dearly and were loyally committed to him. All of them—like Wesley— were willing to live or die in the pouring out of their lives for Christ. Understandably, Methodism grew and spread rapidly.

For 53 years, Wesley himself traveled a quarter of a million miles taking the message of salvation to the people of England—primarily on foot or horseback. He sometimes preached five to six times a day. When he died at age 88, he had completed a preaching mission only two weeks before. He gave his absolute best effort for Jesus Christ to the very end.

William Wilberforce (1759–1833)

The Evangelical Revival of eighteenth century England awakened the moral conscience of many people of wealth and influence. Among these, William Wilberforce and a group of his peers banded together to rid the world of slavery starting in England. These twelve dedicated Christian professionals gave their greatest attention and energy to seeing transformation occur at various levels in their nation.

The dedication to their cause by this group was intense. One of them lost a substantial part of his fortune, one contributed 80% of his income to charity, and numbers of them were hounded unmercifully by public criticism and malicious slander. Wilberforce himself suffered a nervous breakdown and the young Prime Minister, William Pitt the Younger (1759–1806), died a premature death in office due to the pressures of his taking up the cause against slavery.

Nevertheless, this revolutionary company of twelve "challenged the whole moral climate of their times and changed their world! Their efforts ranged across a wide spectrum of issues including slavery, missions, prison reform, public immorality, and the needs of the poor." [4] They single-handedly were responsible for the English Parliament officially abolishing the slave trade and emancipating all British slaves.

These Christian revolutionaries demonstrated the difference a handful of believers with Jesus' revolutionary spirit can make in effecting moral and social changes in a nation. They were committed to one another as a community, apart from which they could not have carried on the battle alone. They refused to accept setbacks as final defeats. They were committed to struggling for the long haul, even if it took decades. They did not let the opponents vicious attacks distract them or provoke them into similar response. They laid their lives on the altar to see God's kingdom come to their nation.[5]

Maria Woodworth-Etter (1844-1924)

This mother of six was a true revolutionary forerunner in America Christianity. Saved as a farm- girl at age 13, Maria Woodworth-Etter heard God call her to preach the gospel. She responded to God's call with radical abandonment and became an extraordinary agent of change. Many hundreds of thousands were saved in response to her preaching that was accompanied by extraordinary healing, signs, and wonders. In spite of being a woman afflicted with continual health problems, she proved to be a powerful woman who would lift her tiny hand and allow the Holy Spirit to spread His fire!

Maria's meetings introduced the manifestations of the Holy Spirit before they were widely known or experienced in the twentieth century. Dramatic healings of the incurably sick occurred in her meetings. Broken bones were instantly mended, the paralyzed walked, the blind saw, the deaf heard and spoke, demons were cast out, and even the dead were raised to life during her ministry.

Maria's preaching (like Paul's) was not with wise and persuasive words, but with *"a demonstration of the Spirit's power"* so that people's faith *"might not rest on men's wisdom but on God's power"* (1 Cor. 2:4–5). As a spiritual revolutionary, her influence pioneered the way for the founding of many Pentecostal denominations.[6] Some believe her ministry was accompanied by more signs and wonders than any messenger since the early church up to that time.

William J. Seymour (1870–1922)

William Seymour was born to parents who were freed slaves, faced the constant pressures of poverty, injustice and racial hatred. William Seymour faced a multitude of daunting challenges to become a revolutionary man of God with extraordinary kingdom influence in his day.

Seymour was blind in one eye (from smallpox) but had sharp and clear spiritual vision. After his conversion, William Seymour was mentored by Charles Fox Parham (1873–1929), one of the first Pentecostal pioneers, who introduced him to the teaching on the baptism in the Holy Spirit with speaking in tongues.

His destiny began to unfold when Seymour went to Los Angeles in the spring of 1906. After being initially rejected by a black Nazarene mission, Seymour took his revolutionary message to a small group of hungry believers on Bonnie Brae Street (in Los Angeles) who began to cry out for the baptism in the Holy Spirit. The Lord responded to their heart cry by baptizing them in the Spirit with speaking in tongues.

When this revolutionary fire fully blazed in the Azusa Street Revival, Seymour endured ridicule from both the world and the church. He was persecuted by the church and its leaders for his "strange" Acts teachings, for the Pentecostal manifestations that regularly occurred at the Azusa Street meetings, for the racial integration of the revival, and for including women in church ministry. Some white leaders distained him because of racial prejudice; other were jealous of his influence.

The church-culture of Los Angeles and beyond was not ready for William Seymour or his message! But this revolutionary forerunner refused to give up! Seymour was carrying fire from heaven that God was about to use to ignite the whole earth. History now credits him as being the foremost catalyst for the global Pentecostal revival that ushered in the next era in redemptive history. Only eternity will reveal the full measure of Seymour's ministry and influence. "He was an able stick of dynamite whom God could use to send the explosions of Pentecostal revival around the world. And he did!"[7]

Dietrich Bonhoeffer (1906–1945)

Dietrich Bonhoeffer, a Lutheran pastor and theologian, was a quiet spiritual revolutionary in Nazi Germany. He came from a distinguished intellectual family of scholars and university professors. He distinguished himself in the academic world until German political authorities forbid him in 1936 to teach any longer.[8] Afterward Bonhoeffer trained ministers in a seminary unapproved by the government. Here he had great influence on young leaders and wrote his revolutionary literature including *The Cost of Discipleship* (1937).[9]

Bonhoeffer felt that what was emerging in Germany was so evil it had to be resisted through the church and a political underground resistance movement. He courageously opposed Hitler and Nazism as "a political system which corrupted and grossly misled a nation and made the 'Fuhrer' its idol and god."[10] For Bonhoeffer, Hitler was the antichrist, the arch-destroyer of the world and the basic values of truth, justice, goodness and decency.

Bonhoeffer was arrested in April 1943 by the Gestapo and imprisoned for eigthteen months in Berlin, during which time he smuggled some of his writings out to the free world. During that time he pastored other prisoners from all over Europe. Here he ministered to the sick, the frightened, and the depressed. His execution by hanging occurred on 9 April 1945, only a few days before the village was liberated by the allied forces.[11]

Bonhoeffer made history by demonstrating authentic discipleship and loyal obedience to Christ at the cost of his life. He understood that loyalty often means suffering for Christ. He considered complacency a great sin against the Holy Spirit, and "regarded ambition and vanity as the start of the road to hell."[12] Bonhoeffer's revolutionary, courageous resistance of Nazism and the moral compromise in the church should inspire all authentic believers in the twenty-first century to be faithful to Jesus Christ in the midst of a compromising church and the global rise of the antichrist spirit.

Spiritual revolutionists disturb and disrupt the status quo as forerunners of spiritual, moral, and social reform in their communities and the nation.

If the church is to see great revival with transformational change happening on a big scale in individual lives, families, neighborhoods, congregations and communities in this generation, it will again require night and day prayer, regular fasting, prophetic intercession, spiritual warfare, holiness unto the Lord, and a Spirit-empowered labor-force of radical spiritual revolutionaries.

The coming revival will also require an army of faithful believers with moral integrity, faith and courage, and the backbone of Bonhoeffer to take their stand with Jesus Christ and for righteousness in an evil and perverse generation.

6

Divine Progression in Great Revivals

*My Father is always at his work to this very day, and I, too,
am working. . . . I tell you the truth, the Son can do nothing
by himself; he can do only what he sees his Father doing.*

John 5:17, 19

God's progressive revelation and the progressive nature
of His redemptive story are important concepts for understanding both biblical revelation and revival history. God
is neither detached from history nor acting arbitrarily through
events in history—i.e., initiating first one thing and then another without foreplanning and purpose. Nor is God reacting
to the forces that are shaping world history, as if taking Him
by surprise.

The hearts of leaders of nations are in the hand of the Lord and
He directs history like a watercourse towards its ultimate direction and conclusion (Prov. 21:1). This does not mean that everything national leaders desire or do come directly from the Lord.
It does mean, however, that God has ultimate authority over the
rulers of the world and at times chooses to influence their deci-
sions directly so as to further His redemptive purpose in history.

Furthermore, the Bible teaches that the prayers of God's
people move God to interfere with evil rulers or to direct the
decision of rulers more fully in accordance with His will (e.g., 1
Tim. 2:1–3). Many are the plans of leaders and rulers of nations,

"but it is the Lord's purpose that prevails" (Prov. 19:21). God is working—intentionally and progressively—toward a specific goal, namely, the full redemption for His creation and the final preparation of the Bride for His Son.

The Bible reveals that history is moving forward in purposeful progression from a God-initiated beginning to a God-appointed end. God transcends history as the Creator, descends into history as the Redeemer, and will return as the Bridegroom to unite with His prepared Bride to rule with Him in an ever increasing and expanding kingdom (Rev. 19:6, 9; 21:7, 9, 10).

In the progressive unfolding of redemptive history toward its end-time goal, revival history plays an important and even crucial role in the outcome. Revival is a catalyst to advance the church from its present state to the next level of restoration on the road to the fullness of God's glory in the earth.

Just as redemption is necessary because of the fall and sinfulness of humanity, so revival is necessary because of the church's tendency to spiritual lethargy and decline! Therefore, God's larger revival purpose must be viewed in the context of redemption, and more specifically in the context of the progressive nature of redemption. A macro read of church history reveals a divine pattern. God has been restoring and shaping the church through the catalytic impact of historic revivals since the Protestant Reformation.

In redemptive history and in revival history—the latter being an important segment of the total redemptive story—there occurs a gradual and progressive unfolding of God's master architectural plan for the people of faith. God's goal in the progressive unfolding of both redemptive and revival history is the restoration of all things spoken of by the prophets (Acts 3:19–21) and the fullness of God's eternal intention for His church, the Bride of Christ.

Progressive Nature of Redemption

God-planned and God-initiated redemption is necessary because of the universality of sin and because of death as the mortal and eternal consequence of sin. Biblical redemption involves past, present, and future history and has its core center in Jesus Christ. Redemptive history and world history are not the same. While God sovereignty transcends world history and directs its outcome like directing a watercourse, redemptive history is uniquely His story.

It is important to understand that God intentionally placed *a progressive element* in the two parts of the total redemptive story that centers in Jesus Christ—involving both biblical history and church history. A holy progression occurs from creation to the cross and from the cross to Jesus' second coming. Between Genesis 3 and Revelation 22, there is clearly a progressively revealed and developed understanding about God and the outworking of His plan in redemptive history. God is *progressively* at work in our fallen world to reveal the grandeur and glory of who He is and to bring forth who He created us to be!

God works progressively in history! God never does everything at once or in a hurry, certainly not in revival history. Like in the building of a home, there is first the clearing of the ground, then follows the laying of the foundation, constructing the framework for the building, enclosing the walls, laying the roof, and finally the finished work occurs on the inside and outside of the house.

God's progressive revelation of Himself by spoken word and by mighty deeds has occurred over a large span of time, rooted in biblical events like the exodus, conquest, Davidic kingdom, exile and return, life-death-resurrection of Jesus, outpouring of the Holy Spirit in Acts, and the expansion of the church throughout the first century. "Progressive" refers to the steady unfolding of God's redemptive story along a divine continuum from its first faint beginnings in Genesis to its glorious fullness in Jesus Christ in the Book of Revelation.

In this progressively unfolding redemptive story from Abraham to the present, an amazing pattern is discernible. The consistent pattern is that a highly significant, new epoch begins every 500 years without exception. The dictionary definition of "**epoch**[1]" is "the beginning of a new and important period in the history of something."

The sequence of these 500 year epochs began approximately 4,000 years ago with Abraham (**2000 BC**), followed by Moses and the Exodus (**1500 BC**), King David (**1000 BC**), the Post-Exilic Jewish Restoration (**500 BC**), the Incarnation of Jesus Christ (**0 BC**), the Formal Institutionalizing of the Church (**AD 500**), the East and the West Division in Christianity (**AD 1000**), the Protestant Reformation (**AD 1500**) and our present hour in redemptive history (**AD 2000**).

When God established His covenant with Abraham, He laid the foundation for later covenants and more complete revelation. Each part of the Old Testament is incomplete, though not incorrect, and looks forward to the time of fullness and fulfillment in Jesus Christ.

God's redemptive story occurs *progressively* in the context of divinely initiated covenants. The framework and context for redemption has always been and presently is covenant relationship with God. All of God's redemptive initiatives, especially those He makes corporately, are in the context of covenant—the Abrahamic covenant, the Mosaic covenant, the Davidic covenant, and finally "the New Covenant" as the ultimate redemptive covenant.

The continuity of God's progressive revelation is evident in that the New Covenant is based on the blood of Jesus Christ— "the Seed of Abraham," the fulfillment of types, and shadows built by God into the Mosaic Covenant (Luke 22:7–8, 14–20; Heb 4:1; 10:18), and the "Son of David" Messiah.

In God's *progressive* unfolding of redemption, fullness began

---

1   *Webster's New World College Dictionary* (4th edition, 2005).

with Christ's first coming and will culminate in His second coming. Between Christ's first and second comings, an ongoing progressive unfolding occurs in church history as God continues to develop and work out on the earth the redemption of the cross.

Men and women from the earliest of time until the present are "links" in the chain of covenant history, partnering with God in His redemptive story. Heroes of faith existed not only in biblical history, but also are found throughout church history and today.

When we talk about the progressive nature of redemption beyond biblical history, we are not suggesting an addition to canonical Scripture. What we are saying is that the redemptive story of God is progressively unfolding until the fullness of it all is finally realized when Jesus Christ returns to the earth.

Progressive Nature of Church History

Since the crucifixion and resurrection of Christ Jesus, God has intended to work through His church as His body and redemptive agent of the kingdom. Our best picture of God's intention is seen in the first century coming of the Lord Jesus Christ and the birth of the early church in the power of the Holy Spirit. After Jesus ascended, His ministry on the earth continued when the Holy Spirit was poured out on the early disciples.

The church then went forth to proclaim the kingdom of God in the same power of the Spirit that Jesus proclaimed the kingdom of God while He was on the earth—the same anointing, the same empowering presence of the Holy Spirit, the same works of power. Jesus had prophesied this when He said: *"I tell you the truth, anyone who has faith in me will do what I have been doing. He will do even greater things than these, because I am going to the Father"* (John 14:12).

The sober truth of church history is that, after the first century, there began to be a gradual decline of the first century anointing, proclamation, and purposes of God for the church. By the year AD 500, the main expression of the church was an organized institution.

Church history comprises the last 2000 years of redemptive history. The great Yale Church historian, Kenneth Scott Latourette (1884–1968), has comprehensively divided church history into three large blocks of time: (1) the first five centuries, (2) the next 1,000 years which historians call the "Dark Ages," and (3) the last five centuries.

The *first* 500 years comprise what Latourette calls "Early Christianity" (AD 30–500). After the first century birth of the church in the power of the Holy Spirit and following the death of John (the last of the twelve apostles), the church began a gradual decline of the presence and power of the Holy Spirit in the life of the church. Dependence upon the gifts and ministry of the Holy Spirit likewise declined. Instead of the church continuing to be pneumatic and fluid as in the beginning, she gradually became an institution with governmental organization that looked like the culture and political systems of the day.

By AD 500, the church was able to perpetuate herself organizationally and no longer rely on the presence, gifts, and power of the Holy Spirit so that the supernatural dimension in the church's life and ministry greatly diminished.

The *next* 1,000 years (AD 500–1500) are called the "Middle Ages" (also called the "Dark Ages") during which Christianity and European/Mediterranean political history merged as an intertwined entity. About AD 1000 the great divorce occurred between Eastern Christianity and Western Christianity, solidifying the great East and West divide politically and culturally that has characterized subsequent world history.

The church's political compromises led to a 1,000 year period of deep spiritual darkness and thus, the name "The Dark Ages." This time was dark especially from a spiritual standpoint. While there remained (during this period) small pockets of life, the mainstream of the church and socio-political world was dark and oppressive.

During this period the church was in a state of political compromise and spiritual darkness. These are the years of the churches' greatest embarrassment with a horrible record of man's inhumanity to man in the name of Christ. During these years we have the Crusades, the Inquisitions, and corruption in the church to oppress the masses of common people. It looked like God's original purpose and witness in the church was being snuffed out in those centuries.

Finally, with the Protestant Reformation, classic revival history begins and marks the beginning of gradual spiritual recovery for the church of all that had been stolen or lost through centuries of decline. As there was a gradual spiritual decline the first 500 years of church history, there has been a gradual spiritual recovery and renewal during the last 500 years of church history.

Because the church at the outset of the AD 1500s had lost its way and was groping in spiritual darkness, society was doing the same. Sin flourished and corruption permeated the socio-political structure and leadership at all levels. In the midst of the darkness and devastation, the common people were ravaged by the ensuing injustice. There was little light, less hope and much despair.

The person of the Holy Spirit was no longer a reality in worship, ministry of the Word, the sacraments, or the life of the believer. The authority of Scripture was replaced by ecclesiastical authority or the authority of the church system. The involvement of all believers in ministry and the life of the church were replaced by professional clergy.

Increasingly the "laity" of the church were boxed into dark confinement without any reality of Jesus Christ and the presence of the Holy Spirit in their life or that of the church. Experiential knowledge of God was replaced by ecclesiastical theology that was irrelevant for the ordinary believer. Christian life then became rules and regulations of a politicized church, without experiential joy or relational knowledge of God Himself.

With these developments, the politicized church became the primary voice of authority rather than biblical revelation or the voice of God. The church and its leaders were controlling and manipulative, keeping the people in darkness and ignorance about the Bible.

As a result, the church lost its fundamental message of justification by faith in Jesus Christ. Salvation was viewed as an issue of works and a merit system. The church was corrupt in numerous ways and exploited the fear of the people by charging them money in exchange for getting loved ones and themselves out of purgatory or eternal punishment.

It was in the midst of this corrupt church system and leadership that Martin Luther nailed his "95 Theses" to the door of the Wittenburg Castle that set in motion the great revolution that we now know as the Protestant Reformation.

The *third* block of church history began with the Reformation and continues to the present. Some refer to this 500 year period as "Modern Christianity." Classic revival history occurs during this last 500 year block of time. (see Church History Chart next page)

Progressive Nature of Revival History

God has been gradually and progressively unfolding His master plan of redemption since He initiated His redemptive covenant with Abraham 4,000 years ago. Within the broad scope of *redemptive history*, God has been at work through *church history*, and through the progressive nature and catalytic impact of *revival history* within the last 500 years of church history since the Reformation.

Just as the revelation of God and His master plan of redemption have been gradually and progressively unfolding since Abraham, God is continuing to unfold that plan through church history. Likewise, God's master plan in classic revival history has been gradually and progressively unfolding since the Reformation 500 years ago.

Although there were occasionally pockets of revival and renewal in Early Christianity and the Middle Ages, classic revivals are a divine-human phenomenon that uniquely characterizes church history since the Reformation.

During the last 500 years since the Reformation, four major "revival eras" have occurred. An "**era**[2]" is defined as "the reckoning of time by numbering the years from some important occurrence or given point of time." It may also be "an event or date that marks the beginning of a new and important period in the history of something."

Within each of the four major revival eras, there are clusters of revivals. Revivals within an era may have some individual features as well as share common features with all classic revivals. But typically revivals within an era also share certain distinct progressive characteristics common to that particular era. It is this *distinctively progressive characteristic of each era* that we will primarily mention, even as we acknowledge some common features do exist among classic revivals in all eras.

In classic revival history (AD 1500–2000), as a new revival era has come and gone, there has been a subsiding but not an annulling of what preceded. What precedes is always foundational to what follows and to what is to come. As one revival era has faded in intensity and impact, a new era has always emerged to advance redemption further along the path toward God's fullness for His church.

All is never lost in the passing of a revival or of a revival era. Each successive revival era has built on what occurred before it. Each previous revival era has become "seed" that

---

2   *Webster's New World College Dictionary* (4th edition, 2005).

3 Major Periods of Church History

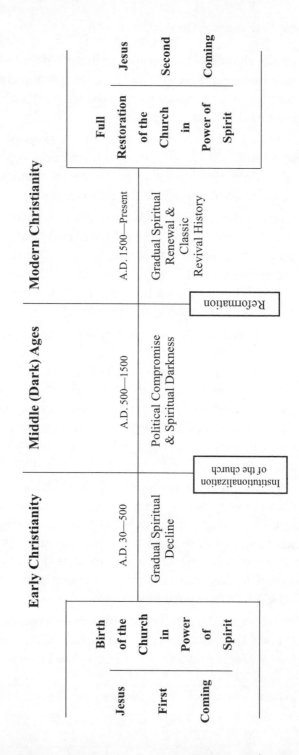

Early Christianity

A.D. 30—500

Gradual Spiritual Decline

Jesus First Coming — Birth of the Church in Power of Spirit

Institutionalization of the church

Middle (Dark) Ages

A.D. 500—1500

Political Compromise & Spiritual Darkness

Reformation

Modern Christianity

A.D. 1500—Present

Gradual Spiritual Renewal & Classic Revival History

Full Restoration of the Church in Power of Spirit — Jesus Second Coming has fallen into the ground and died so that there could be a harvest in the next revival era. Seed sown in a previous era, eventually sprouts and brings forth fruit and more fruit in the next new era. This is in keeping with God's overall goal of: (1) progressively bringing His church in the earth *"to the whole measure of the fullness of Christ"* (Eph. 4:13); and (2) of reaping a fullness of harvest among the nations in all the earth.

Major Revival Eras

On this redemptive continuum of revival history, the following four major eras of classic revival have occurred since AD 1500.

Classic Revival Era 1: The Reformation Era (AD 1500–1699)

Although the Protestant Reformation Era was largely theological and doctrinal in nature, it was accompanied by a new spiritual climate with emphasis on saving faith, the authority of Scripture, priesthood of all believers, the preaching of the gospel, and the appearance of new song and inspired music as an expression of fresh life, joy and worship. All subsequent revivals have been characterized by these major themes.

The preaching of the Bible and of salvation through faith in Jesus Christ alone was like the loosing of redemptive fire from heaven in sixteenth century Europe, making possible the beginnings of spiritual revivals in this era. Revival fires began to burn among the Anabaptists in Germany, Switzerland, and Holland; the Puritans in England and the British Isles; and the early Pietistic revivals in Germany and other parts of Europe. These revivals redefined how people are saved and clearly identified who the people of God are.

Among the first of these revival movements were the *Anabaptists*, a radical wing of the Reformation in Europe. Instead of focusing on changing doctrines and church practices like other reformers, the Anabaptists emphasized spiritual conversion and the changing of people's lives through the power of Jesus Christ. Revivals often broke out wherever they went and large numbers of people were converted. The Anabaptists became a large movement that emphasized the authority of Scripture over ecclesiastical authority, the new birth in Christ, and a life of humility and holiness for converts. Their transformed lives exemplified love, faith, and the power of the cross. Hundreds of them died as martyrs, patiently steadfast in their faith in spite of severe persecution.

In sixteenth century England, the Enlightenment had a severely negative impact on the church. Gradually rationalism replaced faith; human authority replaced God's authority in Scripture; and a secular view of society replaced God and the church as the focal point of life. During this era of "spiritual identity crisis,"[1] God raised up a major revival movement called **English Puritanism**. Numerous dissenting preachers emerged who sought to purify the established church and thus, their name "Puritans."

Puritan preachers emphasized the authority of Scripture, spiritual conversion to Christ, and living a holy life. Their preaching was often accompanied by an anointing and power of the Holy Spirit unknown before in the church. God began to do the same in other parts of England through similar anointed preaching until there were revival fires burning in the British Isles.

One fiery Puritan preacher and writer in England was John Bunyan (1628–1688), author of *The Pilgrims Progress*.

Eventually a group of Puritans immigrated to America on the *Mayflower* ship, landing at Plymouth Rock, Massachusetts in December 1620. These "Pilgrim Fathers" laid the foundations for revival and subsequent spiritual awakenings in Colonial America. Jonathan Edwards (1703–1758) was in this Puritan stream in New England.

A similar revival movement called *Pietism* occurred in Lutheran and Reformed churches in Europe in the 1600s. The Lutheran church in Europe after the death of Martin Luther focused on right doctrine ("orthodoxy") but neglected spiritual conversion, prayer, the Bible, fervent preaching, communion with God, and holy living. Pietism was a people's movement that arose initially as a reaction to the cold orthodoxy of Lutheranism.

As a "new Lutheran bolt of lightening,"[2] Pietism emphasized the new birth experience, the Lordship of Christ, the authority of God's word, and the importance of spiritual vitality and faith. The revival began through biblical preaching, organized prayer meetings, and Bible studies for new believers. This revival spread to some of the German Universities and resulted in a powerful renewal movement.

Count Nikolaus Ludwig von Zinzendorf, the founder of the Moravians, had his spiritual foundations in the Pietistic revival in Germany. Out of this revival came a new focus through the Moravians on the importance of intercessory prayer, Christian community, and foreign missions.

Classic Revival Era 2: Great Evangelical Awakenings (AD 1700-1799)

This revival era is the first in church history since New Testament times to result in widespread salvation and spiritual awakening. This second era included a full-blown European Pietistic Revival, the Moravian Revival led by Count Zinzendorf, the Wesleyan Revival in England, and the First Great Awakening in Colonial America with Jonathan Edwards (1703–1758) and George Whitefield.

The revivals during the second era went a step further on the progressive path of revival history than the Protestant Reformation had gone. The Great Evangelical Awakenings of the 1700s were characterized by powerful preaching, crisis conversion, understanding the new birth, and experiential salvation generally.

During the First Great Awakening in Colonial America, George Whitefield preached in the American colonies from 1738–1740 with explosive anointing and power. Whitefield was a weeping, passionate, eloquent preacher from England, whom some have called the most powerful preacher ever. His preaching resulted in thousands of people experiencing a new birth conversion. Jonathan Edwards, a pastor in a Congregational Church in Massachusetts, was leader of the Awakening in New England and the most influential theologian of this revival era in America.

The converts from the preaching of Edwards and Whitefield were incorporated into the status quo church system of the day. Although their preaching laid the foundation for an assault on the church's status quo, the status quo was not directly challenged until America's Second Great Awakening in the 1800s! Consequently the First Great Awakening in America was short-lived.

George Whitefield later expressed regret toward the end of his ministry that he had followed this course instead of, like John Wesley, placing his revival converts in a new wineskin where they could be discipled and their spiritual life and fervor could be sustained over a long period of time.

Some American college revivals during the First Great Awakening became contagious centers of spiritual fire that spread to churches and communities. College campus revivals are a phenomena that have occurred periodically in American revival history, even in recent decades. Though college revivals are catalytic and contagious centers of spiritual fire when they occur, they are typically short-lived as was the case in the First Great Awakening.

By late eighteenth century the spiritual condition on American college campuses—like Yale where genuine revival had previously occurred—was again in an ungodly state. What was true at Yale in New Haven (Connecticut) was also true at other Ivy League colleges. Harvard, Yale, Dartmouth, and Princeton—initially established as training centers for ministers and for spreading the gospel—progressively became seed beds of emerging humanism and atheism.

During the last decade of the eighteenth century, the typical Harvard student was an atheist. Some historians have called the last two decades of the eighteenth century one of the darkest periods—spiritually and morally—in the history of American Christianity until recent times.

This disturbing situation was suddenly reversed with powerful campus revivals! Students who had no interest in God whatsoever were suddenly awakened and convicted of their sin, encountered God and experienced His forgiveness. One of the most dramatic consequences of college revivals (in all eras) is that many young adults volunteer and dedicate their lives for missions. Campus revivals have always contributed to societal transformation by helping shape spiritually-minded leaders for the next generation.[3]

Bernard Bailyn (1922 –), winner of the Pulitzer Prize for research in American Colonial History, called the First Great Awakening "the central event in the history of religion in America in the eighteenth Century." This movement aroused a spirit of humanitarianism, encouraged the notion of equal rights, and inspired the American Revolution with feelings of democracy.[4]

Classic Revival Era 3: Deeper Life Awakenings (AD 1800–1899)

The experiential nature of the Evangelical Awakenings in the eighteenth century paved the way for the Deeper Life Awakenings in the nineteenth century, both of which prepared the way for the Holy Spirit outpourings in the twentieth century.

The Deeper Life Awakenings in the nineteenth century focused not only on an evangelical conversion experience, but also on the inner life issues of the converted. The one major exception to this pattern was the Prayer Meeting Revival 1857–1859 that began in New York City and spread to other major American cities, impacting most mainline denominational churches with new spiritual life and new converts.

The more characteristic Deeper Life Awakenings of this third revival era included the revivals of William and Catherine Booth and their Salvation Army in England; Andrew Murray and the revivals in South Africa; the revivals of Charles Finney, the Methodists and Frontier Camp Meetings; the Holiness Movement in America; and the Keswick Movement in the latter part of nineteenth century England and America. These revivals were confrontational with the status quo and called for radical conversions and sanctified disciples. The leaders of these awakenings believed they were heralding and building God's kingdom on the earth.

These Deeper Life Awakenings went a step further along the path of restoring the church to New Testament Christianity than the Evangelical Awakenings had gone in the previous century. These revivals all emphasized the sanctification of the believer, both in terms of an experiential encounter with God's sanctifying power as well as a progressive development of the inner spiritual life. These deeper life movements emphasized being filled with the Holy Spirit subsequent to conversion but in a pre-Pentecostal way.

The social impact of this revival era during the pre-Civil War days has been documented by Timothy L. Smith in an award winning book, *Revivalism & Social Reform.* Smith carefully documents the massive societal implications of the national revivals during this important century in United States history.

Classic Revival Era 4: Global Outpouring of the Holy Spirit (AD 1900–1999)

The twentieth century was the first century in which historic revivals became global in their presence and impact. Previously, revivals were regional, national, or confined largely to one continent.

The Fourth Major Revival Era began with the Welsh Revival (1904–06), a revival that spread rapidly to the nations in an unprecedented way. This was quickly followed by the Azusa Street outbreak in Los Angeles and the Pentecostal outpourings of the Holy Spirit on every continent.

The Azusa Street Revival (1906–08) was the most catalytic spiritual event of the twentieth century and perhaps the most influential revival of all time. The Lord took up residency on the earth 1906–1909 at 312 Azusa Street, Los Angeles, California! God's presence caused a great stir in the City of Los Angeles, surrounding communities, and eventually the whole world. The revival was birthed through an African-American pastor named William Seymour as an unlikely vessel in an unlikely setting!

Azusa Street was welcomed by many as a second Pentecost but was harshly criticized by others who opposed what was occurring. The Los Angeles Times newspaper (18 April 1906) on its front page had an article titled, "The Happenings at Azusa Street," which referred to the revival as a weird babble of tongues, the breaking loose of a new sect of fanatics and the mouthing of a creed which no sane mortal could understand.

Dr. P. F. Bresee (1838–1915), pastor in Los Angeles of the mother church of the emerging Nazarene denomination, wrote in the 13 December 1906 edition of *The Nazarene Messenger* that "speaking in tongues" at the Azusa Street Revival was senseless mumbling, and that the various manifestations there were unsanctified fanaticism, strange fire, and heretical teaching.[5]

Other similar fiery missiles were hurled at Seymour and the revival. Nevertheless, within a few years this revival had circled the globe touching multiple millions and birthing many new denominations and ministries—thus transforming the face of Christendom forever! The new denominations formed—including the Assemblies of God—impacted the world extensively in the next few decades by sending large numbers of missionaries to the nations.

The revival itself was marked by an unprecedented outpouring of the Holy Spirit like in the Book of Acts with speaking in tongues, dramatic healings, and great salvation. The manifest presence of God was oftentimes like a cloud in the meetings, sometimes so thick children would play "hide-and-seek" in it. In this heavy presence of God, powerful healings and notable miracles would occur and conviction would fall on even the harshest critic. Numerous times people witnessed the fire of God resting over the Azusa Street building as if the roof were ablaze, while inside the power of God was present to heal, save, and deliver!

In the midst of this great outpouring of the Holy Spirit and miraculous gifts, the focus of the revival remained on Jesus and the revelation of God's love. People were encouraged not only to seek the baptism in the Holy Spirit with the evidence of tongues but more importantly to seek Jesus Himself. The spiritual atmosphere was electric with God's presence, and charged with an awe and fear of God.

Azusa Street became a "fountainhead of Pentecost" for the entire world. Seymour and others in the revival believed that God was pouring out His Spirit to evangelize the world before the Lord would return. Subsequent history is vindicating this prophetic anticipation.

Even in the earliest days of the revival, many seemed aware that this revival would spread and impact the world for Christ. This conviction alone led to many missionaries leaving Azusa

Street to serve in other nations. Within a few years the revival had spread to 50 nations—making it and the Welsh Revival the first truly global revivals the church ever experienced.

The subsequent decades of the fourth revival era (twentieth century) continued to focus on the Holy Spirit's ministry and gifts in the progressive journey of bringing the church fully back to her Book of Acts origin. A scholar and historian, Harold Vinson Synan (1931–), refers to the twentieth century as the "Century of the Holy Spirit."[6] The Charismatic Movement brought the Pentecostal message and experience of the Holy Spirit into the mainstream of Protestantism and the Roman Catholic Church throughout the world. No less than 520 million persons have been spiritually impacted by the Pentecostal and Charismatic revivals worldwide.

Harvey Gallagher Cox (1929–), a Harvard professor, wrote a book in 1994 that described and analyzed the global Pentecostal revival in the twentieth century. In contrast to his colleagues at Harvard, Cox believes—after his research and writing the book—that the church is on the verge of another worldwide spiritual revival. He chastises those in the academic community who have predicted the decline and demise of Christianity.

Cox describes the twentieth century Pentecostal/Charismatic Revival as a "spiritual hurricane" that impacted at least half a billion people worldwide.[7] The catalytic nature of revival in this fourth era has been so extensive that it has altered the expression and understanding of Christianity in one century!

For good reason the twentieth century is being called the "Century of the Holy Spirit." The century began with the Holy Spirit breaking out in revivals (like the Welsh and Azusa Street Revivals) all over the world, on every continent. Latin America, England, Australia/New Zealand, Europe, Asia, and Africa have all been greatly impacted by the Holy Spirit's presence and power.

In China, the Holy Spirit broke out in the context of post-1949 traditional evangelical missionary work. Without any theological education or formal teaching, the underground church in China after communism's domination and persecution has emerged looking like the Book of Acts because of the Holy Spirit's activity there!

In the world-wide revival of the Holy Spirit, the church rediscovered the third person of the Godhead along with His presence and power. This revival and rediscovery of the Holy Spirit world-wide has included His healing, gifts, miracles, and power-evangelism in unprecedented ways since the first century.

This Fourth Major Revival Era enabled the church to make a major advance forward along the progressive path of restoring the church back to New Testament Christianity. Moreover, the spiritual, moral, and social impact of this revival era has not only been global in scope, it also continues to bear fruit worldwide.

Restoration in Revival History

Following 1,000 years of spiritual darkness, devastation, and injustice, God intervened and challenged the corrupt church and its leaders with the power of His Word. The spiritual explosion that followed in the Reformation rocked the world and changed the course of church history forever! From that point God began to restore to His church one layer after another of His kingdom reality, of understanding biblical truth and of experiential knowledge of Him.

The Reformation is a critical "hinge" point of history and launched—among other things—500 years of on-going revival history, with each revival era bringing another level of restoration to the church.

The Lord dramatically impacted church history in the

Reformation by restoring the truth of salvation by grace to the church. God began by restoring first things first: first, justification is by faith, not by works; then God focused on the experiential realities in conversion and new birth with multitudes coming to Christ in the *great Evangelical Awakenings* that followed. In the *Deeper Life Awakenings*, God added to the conversion experience of believers revelatory understanding of the sanctification of the believer as another essential biblical truth and reality of the Christian life.

In the twentieth century God restored to the church the person of the Holy Spirit with not only His fruit but also His gifts; the supernatural presence and power that had been lost since the early church. This spiritual explosion restored so much of what we now take for granted as "normal" Christian experience and ministry.

The Azusa Street Revival and the worldwide outpouring of the Holy Spirit that followed marked another important shift and hinge point in church history, similar in scope and significance to the Reformation in the sixteenth century.

Whereas the Reformation restored the basic message of the gospel—*the Word*, the Pentecostal outpouring restored *the Spirit* with power to complete the Great Commission among the nations. This is the same sequence that we find in the New Testament. First, Jesus as the Word came and established the message of the gospel. After Jesus' death, resurrection, and ascension, the Holy Spirit was given in power to believers for proclaiming the message of the gospel to the nations.

The Lord rebaptized the church with the Holy Spirit to recommission the church to take the gospel of the kingdom to the nations. This assignment had been hindered during the previous 1,400 years because of the absence of the Holy Spirit's presence and power. After Azusa Street, the gospel of the kingdom spread quickly like fire to 50 nations and then beyond.

God's progressive redeeming activity in each successive revival era has and will play an important role in bringing the redemptive story to fullness and the church to the fullness of her destiny in Christ. Considering what God has already done in the previous four revival eras, what does God have in mind for the *next* (and likely final) revival era? (see Redemption Chart next page)

The Journey Continues

As we get closer to the end of the age and redemption's culmination, the journey will look much different than in previous generations. In the twenty-first century, God is transitioning the church to something new in His emerging progressive plan!

God is not "recycling" history by repeating revivals! God doesn't go in circles in His workings in history. God is linear in His plan! By this we mean He is purposefully moving human and redemptive history from a beginning to a conclusion. God is taking us somewhere!

God's redemptive strategy is progressively moving the church forward toward Jesus' return to earth. Redemptive history is progressive! Revival history is progressive! Therefore, we cannot just wait in the twenty-first century and hope for a revival like we have read about or seen in the past!

While we should treasure and spiritually profit from what God has done previously, we must not "park" at previous spiritual landmarks. The tendency to "park" spiritually, theologically, or experientially can become an obstacle to our *continuing* on the progressive journey with God. If we "park" and do not continue with God on the journey forward, we will miss our destiny and likely oppose the next revival era. We all face this question, "Will we move forward with God in this present generation?"

If we do not continue to make the journey forward with God

in this generation, we will end up setting on the sideline (probably as a critic), watching at a distance the new era that God unfolds. God never stops "working" and moving toward fullness! We are living in a day of unprecedented activity of God across the earth in ways we never could have imagined. We can rightly anticipate a restoration increase of God's manifest presence and glory in the next revival era of redemptive history!

The Redemptive Story Line—Progression in 500 Year Epochs

Scope of Church History—Jesus' Ascension to His Return

Restoration of the Church In Major Revival Eras

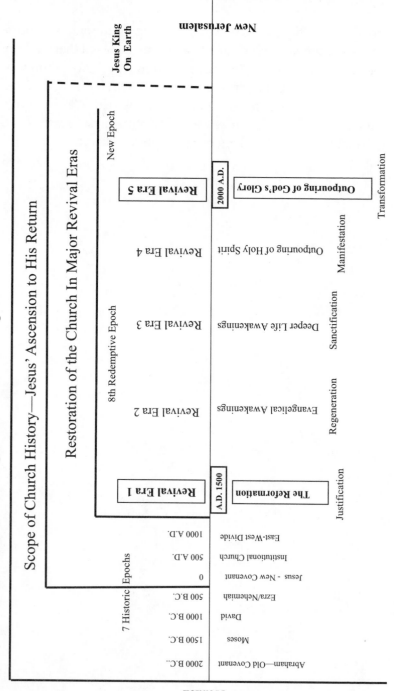

Creation								

New Jerusalem

Jesus King On Earth

New Epoch

8th Redemptive Epoch

Revival Era 5 — 2000 A.D. — Outpouring of God's Glory — Transformation

Revival Era 4 — Outpouring of Holy Spirit — Manifestation

Revival Era 3 — Deeper Life Awakenings — Sanctification

Revival Era 2 — Evangelical Awakenings — Regeneration

Revival Era 1 — A.D. 1500 — The Reformation — Justification

7 Historic Epochs

1000 A.D.	East-West Divide
500 A.D.	Institutional Church
0	Jesus - New Covenant
500 B.C.	Ezra/Nehemiah
1000 B.C.	David
1500 B.C.	Moses
2000 B.C.	Abraham—Old Covenant

Part Two

Emerging Revival
& the Future

7

Convergence & Emergence

See, I am doing a new thing!
Now it springs up; do you not perceive it?
Isaiah 43:19

I n the twenty-first century, God is transitioning the church
to something very new in His progressive plan to sum up
all things in Christ! God is moving His church forward to prepare her for fullness at the end of the age.

In the sweep of the past 4,000 years of redemptive history,
an amazing pattern is discernible. The consistent pattern is
that every 500 years another new and highly significant epoch
of redemptive history begins. Every 500 years a new catalytic
leader or major event arises that defines the centuries that follow until another major catalytic person or event appears that
defines the centuries that follow it.

For example, the covenant with Abraham which occurred
around **2000 BC** dominated redemptive history for 500 years
until another highly significant epoch began with Moses and
the exodus around *1500 BC*. The influence of Moses and the
law were the exclusive focus for Israel for centuries. Then 500
years later, God added King David in *1000 BC* and Israel's
monarchy as a prototype of Jesus and His kingdom.

The pattern of major epochs occurring throughout redemptive history highlights the importance of our present hour in

history! In the year 2000 AD we completed another 500 year period of time since the Protestant Reformation in 1500 AD. If this pattern remains consistent, we are now entering another *major catalytic redemptive epoch* that will define the important years that are to follow.

Simultaneously, we have progressively moved through 4 revival eras that have brought great restoration to the church since the Reformation. As we entered the twenty-first century, there is global evidence that a *fifth major revival era* is beginning to emerge.

The fact that the passing of a 500 year period of time and the emergence of a new revival phenomenon are both occurring at the outset of the twenty-first century, highlights the importance of our hour in God's redemptive storyline. This unique convergence of another redemptive epoch and a new revival era indicates that we are living in a strategically significant *chronos and kairos hour!* (See Revival Era Chart on next page).

Signs of Divine Convergence

What does this convergence of a *new redemptive epoch* and a *new revival era* mean? First it means we are in a time of major transition. Five hundred years ago the first convergence of a redemptive epoch and a revival era marked the beginning of the Reformation and of classic revival history for the church.

What is now occurring 500 years later is perhaps no less significant for the church than was the Reformation when the first convergence of a new redemptive epoch and a new revival era occurred. Just as the Reformation was a time of great shifting, so the present hour is a time of great change for the church, society, community, and the land.

Contemporary indicators and signs worldwide suggest that the culmination of redemption is approaching. As we move forward toward redemption's end-time goal, this new

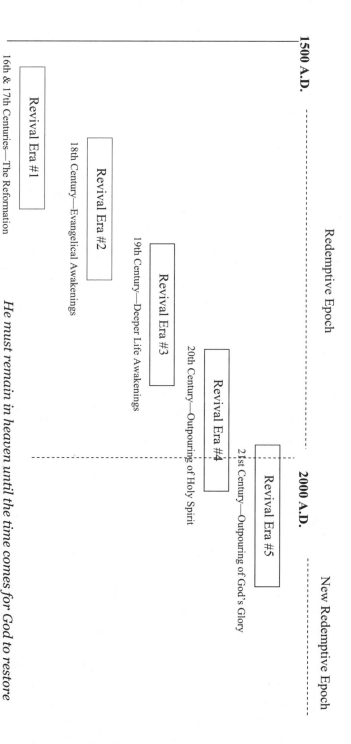

Restoration of the Church In Revival History

1500 A.D.

2000 A.D.

Redemptive Epoch

New Redemptive Epoch

16th & 17th Centuries—The Reformation

Revival Era #1

18th Century—Evangelical Awakenings

Revival Era #2

19th Century—Deeper Life Awakenings

Revival Era #3

20th Century—Outpouring of Holy Spirit

Revival Era #4

21st Century—Outpouring of God's Glory

Revival Era #5

He must remain in heaven until the time comes for God to restore everything, as he promised long ago through his holy prophets.
(Acts 3:21)

revival era may be the last era of revival and redemption. If so, we can be sure that God is going to transform His true church—the Bride of Christ—from her present state to the next level of restoration on the road to the fullness of God's glory in the earth.

In the present transition, numerous global shifts are occurring. *First*, there is an unprecedented worldwide focus on prayer as a fresh **prayer and worship movement** has sprung up simultaneously all over the earth. Corporate 24/7 prayer is growing and intensifying among the nations. People everywhere—in *houses of prayer*, the annual *Global Day of Prayer* with millions of participants in over 200 nations, solemn assemblies like *The Call*, and untold numbers of prayer gatherings in homes, huts and tents, churches, community-wide locations—are praying, watching, and waiting. Arising from the earth is unprecedented and passionate intercession for unprecedented revival and spiritual harvest in the context of the coming unprecedented turmoil.

Second, at the turn of the century, a new **healing movement** began rising in the earth. The John G. Lake healing rooms in Spokane, Washington were reopened in 1999, followed by healing rooms appearing around the world under various organizations. Many major cities of the world now have at least one center for healing prayer. Prayer for the sick and release of the power of God for physical healing—a core reality of the kingdom of God—is experiencing a major revival throughout the earth.

Third, another global phenomenon that has emerged at the turn of the century is the **global missions movement** involving numerous missional streams cooperating together to formulate a strategy for completing the great commission. This unprecedented missions cooperation is for the explicit purpose of developing a shared strategy for presenting Jesus to every unreached-people group and every unevangelized neighborhood in the world.

Fourth, there is a new **global focus of intercession for Israel** by Christians on all continents. In contrast to replacement theology, there is a new global awareness among believers about God's unique destiny for Israel in the end time. Numerous houses of prayer in Jerusalem as well as among the nations are focusing intercession on revival for Israel. Asians, especially Chinese, and Korean missionaries have been compelled by the Lord to "return to Jerusalem" by preaching the gospel along the "Silk Road" to Muslim populations, bringing the message of Christ full circle to Jerusalem where it all began.

The *fifth* important global movement that has been emerging at the turn of the century is the **global transformation movement.** Supernatural transformation is occurring among the nations today that displays God's extravagant redemption for people and for creation, enabling *"the knowledge of the glory of God"* (Hab. 2:14) to spread over the whole earth (Psa. 57:5, 11). This movement, like the previous four, is related to revival—preparing the Bride and reaping the global harvest of salvation at the end of the age.

New Dimension of Revival!

In the twenty-first century we have entered a new era of revival which includes supernatural transformation of entire communities as a stunning reality. Although societal impact is not "new" in classic revival history, we certainly have not seen the astonishing extent of transformation in multiple spheres of society before—including ecology— in many non-Western nations.

Transforming revival—like former classic revivals that have impacted society—is part of God's progressively unfolding, redemptive story. In previous classic revivals, we saw a *measure* of transformation at a community level. In the twenty-first century we are beginning to see transformation as a *major* component of the revivals that are now emerging in many communities among the nations.

A stunning example of supernatural transformation of an entire community is Almolonga, Guatemala. The revival in Almolonga resulted in phenomenal *transformation* of individuals, their families, and every sphere of the community of 20,000 people. Even the physical land itself was dramatically healed.

Almolonga experienced the transforming impact of the manifest presence of God which brought supernatural, measurable, and long lasting change to the people and every level of their society. The community may not be *perfect*, but the transformation is so pervasive it hardly resembles its former condition.

Before its transforming revival, Almolonga was a typical Mayan community steeped in idolatry, poverty, and spiritual darkness. The town was hostile to the gospel, and the worship of spirits dominated the culture. The community was filled with domestic violence, four overcrowded jails, alcohol addiction, deprivation, and dry-barren land. The people sought relief from the pain of their devastation by turning to alcohol and to a local idol named "Maximon." The spirit behind the worship of Maximon had held the community in its power for hundreds of years.

But a pastor and his small congregation, under death threats, became desperate for God and began to pray and fast with great fervency with faith that God would change their entire community. They humbly cried out to God during evening prayer vigils for Him to come in His power to break the power of darkness and the stronghold of Maximon.

They repented of the long-standing community covenant with Maximon and renounced it openly. They resisted the enemy in their midst and the devastating consequences of his presence among them. The first evidence that God was responding to their faith-filled prayers was people began being healed and delivered of demonic oppression and affliction. Many were saved and became transformed disciples of Jesus.

As transforming revival continued, entire families were transformed by the power of God. The many transforming miracles of healing and deliverance have caused Almolonga to be called the "City of God" and "the Valley of Miracles." Today, over 90 percent of the people of Almolonga are Bible-believing Christians. When entering Almolonga on the main road, one passes underneath a banner with big bold print that says, "*Jesus is Lord of Almolonga!*"

Almolonga is a transformed community! It's four jails were closed due to lack of crime. The 30-plus bars have nearly all closed, and now the town is filled with churches. The life of the community—the families, agriculture, businesses, etc.— centers around the life of the church.

The Lord not only saved and healed the people, He also healed the land as in His promise in 2 Chronicles 7:14—"*and will heal their land.*" Now known as "America's vegetable garden," Almolonga's fertile valley produces vegetables of biblical proportions—carrots the size of a man's forearm, radishes as large as a fist, and cabbages as large as basketballs. Productivity of the land has increased a thousand percent. As a result of their abundance, they are providing vegetables for neighboring communities and other countries in Central and South America.

If you walk the streets of Almolonga, as we have done, you can sense the resting presence and peace of God everywhere. People are joyfully working and praising God as they go. Families are restored and the faces of children shine with the joy of the Lord! The marketplace is filled with an abundance of nutritious produce and with people whose lives overflow with God's love and joy.

Visiting a community saturated with the presence of God—where almost the entire community is saved, where

God's glory is evident on the faces of the people, where jails are now used for other purposes due to lack of crime, and the land itself is bursting with life—was beyond what most of us had ever considered possible, at least in our present age.

The transformation miracle of Almolonga was first documented by The Sentinel Group in its first video (1999) entitled *Transformation I*. The documentary shocked the church-world concerning how far God was willing to go with His transforming power as Jesus impacted not only the church but also every community sphere in Almolonga.[1]

God's Glory Spreads

When transformation first appeared in Almolonga (1990s), it was apparent that God was "doing a new thing" in the earth. In a sense, the Almolonga Revival was a "first fruits" offering to the LORD, a revival which contained the spiritual DNA that is now characterizing the transforming revivals of the twenty-first century.

At the beginning of the twenty-first century, *eight communities* were identified as being supernaturally transformed. As of this writing, almost *1,000 communities in 45 nations* represented on every continent have been impacted by the fire of transforming revival in just one decade! In some nations, clusters of transformed communities are multiplying rapidly. In Fiji, the Amazon, Papua New Guinea, and the Canadian Arctic there are dozens of *entire villages* that have experienced salvation and transformation accompanied by signs and wonders and healing of their defiled land. The wide-spread phenomena of supernatural, transforming revival is observable, measurable, and compelling evidence that God is truly orchestrating a new thing in the earth.

That first *Transformation* documentary which featured the transformation of Almolonga was quickly followed by a second documentary, *Transformation 2*. This documentary portrays similar transforming revivals in the Arctic and several other communities in the world. A third documentary followed, *Let the Seas Resound*, which highlighted the transforming revival occurring on a national level in the nation of Fiji. Following the Fiji documentary, another documentary, *An Unconventional War*, tells the heart-wrenching story of the 19–year campaign of terror in Northern Uganda and the powerful breakthrough that occurred as a result of desperate prayer and repentance. Then, *A Force for Change* was released, which features the amazing transformation that is occurring in neighborhoods in Sao Paulo, Brazil led by the Sao Paulo police department!

Most recently, *An Appalachian Dawn* was released, which features the dramatic transformation of a city in the United States. The city is Manchester, Kentucky where drug addiction was rampant, poverty was spiraling out of control, corrupt community officials were being bought off by drug dealers and the churches were divided. One day pastors began to pray and repent together and said "enough!" The change that has occurred since May 2004 is a testimony to God's faithfulness to respond to desperate praying people.

Preeminence of God's Glory

This frequency of supernaturally transformed communities around the world indicates God wants to do more than revive His church. God clearly wants to transform the church and the communities we live in! When God's presence and the Holy Spirit's power greatly impacts the church, the revived church is then prepared to greatly impact society.

Among the observable evidence of God's glory being openly and measurably manifested are entire communities and villages getting saved, signs and wonders occurring both in the heavens and on the earth, the healing of the land itself, and ecological miracles.[2]

God poured out His Spirit globally in the twentieth century, and it became known as the "Century of the Holy Spirit." Could it be that the twenty-first century will be known as the "Century of God's Glory" —the century when the knowledge of God's glory will cover the earth as the waters cover the sea (Hab. 2:14)? The supernatural transformation testimonies in the first decade of this century indicate unprecedented activity of God on the earth.

We are calling this unprecedented activity a fifth revival era. This young era's distinguishing feature so far is new levels of God's glory being manifest globally in an explosion of transforming revivals. This new revival fire is already spreading among the nations and touching every continent with awareness of God's glory. God's plan before Christ returns involves filling the earth with a global testimony and knowledge of His glory (Hab. 2:14).

Prophetic Picture

The Old Testament Tabernacle reminds us of God's intention to dwell in the midst of His redeemed people, to display His glory, and to be worshipped forever. The Tabernacle is a prophetic picture of both heavenly worship and the redemptive story on earth.

The Tabernacle is a prophetic picture that foreshadowed God becoming flesh in His Son and dwelling among men incarnate (John 1:14). It is commonly understood that the Tabernacle furnishings are in the shape of the cross and represent God's redemption on the earth. It also foreshadows the consummation of redemption when Jesus returns and once again God's presence and glory dwells among His people in the New Jerusalem (Rev. 21:22–22:6). The Tabernacle is, therefore, a prophetic object lesson of the redemptive story.

The furnishings of the Tabernacle are in a prescribed order by God and represent things that are true in heaven and in the outworking of God's redemption on the earth. In that sense it also provides a clear illustration of the sequence of the activity of God in revival eras in church history.

In so doing, God gives us a picture that helps us to understand what has already occurred, where we currently are and what He is planning in the future. The Tabernacle gives biblical weight to the sequence of things we should expect in the next redemptive epoch and the fifth revival era. The Tabernacle, given explicitly by God to help us understand things that we otherwise cannot understand, is a prophetic picture that helps us understand what we are to expect.

The first furnishing of the Tabernacle was the Brazen Altar. The Brazen Altar was used for blood sacrifice—for a sin offering. The Brazen Altar corresponds to the emphasis of the Protestant Reformation (sixteenth to seventeenth centuries) on Jesus blood sacrifice and justification by faith. The first revival era (during the Reformation) restored the "altar" to the church—understanding the centrality of the blood of Jesus as our only propitiation for sin.

The second Tabernacle furnishing was the Laver, used for cleansing by the priests as ceremonial preparation for ministry in the presence of God. This corresponds to the Evangelical Revival (eighteenth century) which emphasized the importance of experiential salvation involving the washing of conscience and the cleansing of the heart from sin. This second revival era went a step beyond the understanding of justification by faith by restoring the experiential dimension of salvation by faith.

Next, there were two furnishings in the Holy Place. On the left, the Lampstand—with seven oil lamps that burned day and night—represented the light of the Holy Spirit's presence and ministry in the midst of God's people. This corresponds to the Deeper Life Awakenings (nineteenth century) with its focus on the believer's inner life (i.e., sanctification and the fruit of the Spirit) and to the global outpouring of the Holy Spirit (early twentieth century) with its focus on the oil of the Spirit. The third and fourth revival eras clearly marked a recovery of the presence and power of the Holy Spirit to the church.

The companion furnishing in the Holy Place on the opposite side was the Table of Showbread. This represented for Israel the fellowship of God that the Holy Spirit made possible with His covenant people. This corresponds to the strong emphasis on the Spirit's gifts, *koinonia* fellowship, and the imminence of God's presence in the midst of His people that the Holy Spirit produced worldwide during the fourth revival era in the twentieth century.

The third furnishing in the Holy Place was the Altar of Incense, positioned directly in front of the veil that separated the Holy Place from the Holy of Holies. The Altar of Incense represented Israel's worship and prayers coming before the presence of God in the Holy of Holies. This corresponds to the revival of Spirit-filled worship and intercession that has restored the Altar of Incense in the church's ministry unto the Lord (especially during the last two decades of the twentieth century).

All the furnishings in the Tabernacle were designed by God to prepare the way for what is behind the Temple veil in the Holy of Holies —i.e., the Ark of the Covenant (God's covenant), the Mercy Seat (God's atonement) and the two gold-sculptured Cherubim (God's glory). The sequence in the Tabernacle, thus culminates in the Holy of Holies where the *glory of God* was most intensely represented.

As the previous Tabernacle furnishings (Brazen Altar, Laver, Lampstand, Table of Showbread, and Altar of Incense) well illustrate sequentially the four revival eras since the Reformation, we can expect the last furnishing of the Tabernacle (the Holy of Holies) sequentially will illustrate the fifth revival era (preeminently God's manifest glory).

As the Holy Spirit and His experiential reality were the

preeminent characteristic of the fourth revival era (Joel 2:28), we believe God's *glory* will be a strong presence and testimony in all the earth as the preeminent characteristic of the fifth revival era (Hab. 2:14). This is precisely what we are witnessing today being poured out among the nations in transforming revival in the twenty-first century!

Perceiving the New Day

The reality of classic revivals and their impact on the church and society is clear from written revival accounts. Based on the promises in God's Word, the reality of a final great revival is likewise very compelling. Rather than looking back through history, we can also look *forward* through revelation of God's word to gain some understanding of what is going to occur as the culmination of redemptive history unfolds.

What about revival in our day? For many it is easier to have faith for what God has *already* done or is *going* to do in the future than to have faith for what He desires to do in *our own generation*. It's more difficult to perceive history as it is being made than to read about it after it has occurred. But for believers who are called to partner with God in *making history*, we must have eyes to see and ears to hear what the Spirit is saying to the church *in our day*.

God is again speaking, as in Isaiah 43:19, *"See, I am doing a new thing! Now it springs up; do you not perceive it?"* In order to present to God a heart of wisdom and intentionally participate in His kingdom in a full way in this generation, it is important to understand the times and season in which we now live (cf. 1 Chr. 12:32).

On our journey toward redemptive history's culmination and completeness, we must recognize and anticipate the increase of God's Holy Spirit activity and ministry on the earth. We must also consider our role as partners with God and active participants in His bringing history to a glorious conclusion, rather than be spectators watching from the sidelines!

It is an incomplete understanding of biblical revelation to believe that history just "winds up" in disaster and destruction. God intends to fulfill every promise and intention in His heart about bringing redemptive history to a complete and eternal conclusion.

Our responsibility as believers is not to simply wait in spiritual passivity as history unfolds, but to participate with joyful and obedient hearts so as to be ready as vessels of honor for the Master's use *in our own generation* (2 Tim. 2:21).

As we get closer to the culmination of redemptive history, the journey will look differently than it has in previous generations and centuries. A new fullness of time and redemption is at hand! God is going to reap a great harvest among the nations and transform His true church—the Bride of Christ—from her present state to the next level of restoration on the road to the fullness of God's glory in the earth.

We are living in a day when God's glory is being revealed across the earth. Transforming revivals now occurring among the nations are revealing God's glory in a new and dramatic way. *"Be exalted, O God, above the heavens; let your glory be over all the earth"* (Psa. 57:5, 11). What does God's glory "over all the earth" look like in our day? God's manifest glory is most clearly seen in extravagant redemption!

8

Great Transforming Revival in 21st Century

*"I will cleanse them from all the sin they have committed against me
and will forgive all their sins of rebellion against me.
Then this city will bring me renown, joy, praise and honor
before all nations on earth that hear of all the good things I do for it;
and they will be in awe and will tremble at the abundant
prosperity and peace I provide for it."*

Jeremiah 33:4–9

The transforming revival occurring in the 21st century is unlike any previous revival era and yet is in continuity with all that has preceded in classic revival history. God is not *recycling* revival history – He is moving history *forward* in purposeful progression through the catalytic, restorative impact of revivals.

As previously noted, past classic revivals and current transforming revivals are both part of one progressively unfolding continuum of the same redemptive story line. God is moving His church toward redemptive fullness at the end of the age. Transforming revival is a new chapter in classic revivals and spiritual awakenings. God is presently restoring another level of spiritual reality to the church, perhaps one never before seen in the church age. When transformational evidence began emerging in the late 1990s, it became clear that revival of the church is not the ultimate goal. God clearly has more in mind than short-lived or localized revival meetings! As in classic revival history, revival is to serve as the catalyst that produces profound impact both in the church and lasting fruit affecting the community at large.

Transforming revival occurring in geographic areas is causing profound and widespread awareness of God's greatness and glory. This impact of God's presence and glory at a corporate, community level will help make possible the vast end–time harvest among the nations before Jesus returns.

The acceleration and pervasiveness of transforming revival occurring in the nations gives us great hope for the extent to which God longs to bring redemptive change *in this age* as first-fruits of the *age to come*.

What is Transforming Revival?

Transforming revival is a *corporate encounter* with a *supernatural God* that is *tangible, measurable, and observable* by all who live at the visitation location. God's presence brings accompanying fruit that characterizes His nature and His heavenly kingdom with transformational changes happening at every level—individuals, families, church, society, and land.

"Transforming revival" refers to the entire process of change a community undergoes as a result of God's manifest presence and subsequent spiritual awakening. Like classic revivals in the four previous eras, transforming revival (fifth era) always impacts both the church and society.

Moreover, it involves an acute awareness of God and His holiness that changes the spiritual climate of a community or region with transformational results. It's a manifestation of God's glory, love, wisdom, and power to people who have intentionally abandoned themselves to prepare for His divine presence.

Transforming revival is a significant invasion of God and

His kingdom to people and the community where they live. Transforming revival is God's *salvation* destroying the works of the devil; His extravagant *grace* replacing poverty and lack; His *justice* conquering injustice; and His *love* bringing life to the brokenness of society.

Theologically, everyone agrees that God *intends* to manifest His kingdom on the earth. Most believers, however, have no expectation of entering into the *experiential reality* of what is believed *theologically* and what is promised *biblically*. As transforming revivals occur in communities today, God is closing the gap between what He has promised in His Word and what believers are experiencing as present reality on the earth.

Transforming revival extends beyond personal salvation to honoring Jesus as the Lord over spheres of society such as education, business, finances, and the land. In transforming revival, God is not just filling big buildings with people, He is also bringing redemption and His kingdom to every sphere— family, church, society, and the physical land itself. This is a radical new dimension in revival!

In communities experiencing transforming revival, there is objective evidence that God and His kingdom are impacting the visited communities with dramatic changes in their spiritual atmosphere and physical environment. This change includes broad-scale salvation in the community, deliverance from demonic oppression, miraculous reduction in addictions and abuse, and many times supernatural transformation of the land itself.

How Does Transforming Revival Occur?

Where transforming revival is occurring, God's activity reveals an interesting pattern. The visitation by the Lord is in *response to a formal invitation by the community in the form of intentional preparation by desperate believers*, not simply a *mysterious eruption* of God's presence.

George Otis, Jr. comments about this pattern:

> Transformed communities do not materialize spontane-
> ously. If they did we might legitimately wonder why an
> omnipotent and ostensibly loving God did not turn the
> trick more often. We would also be left to ponder our own
> value as intercessors. Fortunately, such thoughts can be
> banished immediately. This is because community trans-
> formation is not an arbitrary event but rather the product
> of a cause and effect process.[1]

Transforming revival occurs as a result of profound obedience to remove every obstacle to God's holy presence. At the
heart of transforming revival is corporate repentance among
desperate people that prepares the way of the Lord to impact
the church and community with His presence and power.

This revival of repentance is preceded by deep humility
and conviction that the problems we face in society are rooted
in spiritual—not simply natural—causes. Seeking God's face
and His divine intervention becomes the highest priority for
the well-being of the people, families, congregations, and the
community.

In every observable transformation story occurring in the
nations today, a similar process has been identified that includes these three distinct and measurable stages: Invitation,
Visitation, and Transformation. While each transformed community is unique in the specific *fruit* that God's redemption
brings to families and society, the *process* by which they got
there is the same in every community.

Each community that has attracted the presence of God has
done so by humbling themselves before the Lord, taking responsibility for their desperate condition, repenting of their sins
corporately, and returning to covenant and intimacy with God.

In response to this intentional process of corporate repentance and renewed covenant, God's manifest presence comes

to the community with a fresh flow of His life and healing! As the spiritual atmosphere begins to change, people are filled with expectation and desire to further prepare the way of the Lord into their families, congregations and communities, removing every offending sin and obstacle to His holy presence.

Then, as God promises in His Word, He *"hears their cry, forgives their sin and heals their land"* (2 Chron. 7:14). We have no record in Scripture or in contemporary testimonies that a *corporate people* has ever returned to the Lord in genuine humility and true repentance that the Lord turned a deaf ear or refused to fulfill His part of the covenant!

How long does this process take? While the time frame for each phase of the process varies, the first phase of preparation varies more than the others because this phase depends wholly upon commitment levels, humility, and the focused resolve of the people. For some communities the struggle for breakthrough can continue for a long period of time until transforming revival becomes their primary focus and priority. In other communities where the leaders and people *abandon* themselves *wholeheartedly* to the preparation process, God faithfully responds!

Societal transformation flows out of a season of preparation and invitation by God's people in response to His initiative. God's supernatural visitation cannot be scheduled on a calendar, *but it can and must be prepared for!* After God *initiates* the process of transforming revival, His presence then *continues* to undergird and sustain the process.

Key Characteristics of Transforming Revival

Though transforming revival shares the common characteristics of classic revival, we are now seeing something qualitatively unique in the twenty-first century. Among the more prominent features of transforming revival are the following:

- manifestation of God's presence at the community level
- an intentional, corporate process of returning to covenant relationship with God
- corporate obedience to God's Word
- measurable and sustained societal impact
- healing of ecology
- re-identification of communities based on God's transforming intervention

Defining Supernatural Transformation

Whereas, "transforming revival" refers to the *overall process* of change that occurs in a spiritual awakening at a societal level, the term "transformation" describes the *impact of the process* manifested in people, families, congregations, community, and land where they live.

The concept of "transformation" is rich in meaning. In Scripture the word "transformation" is *metamorphos* (Greek) and refers to a process of change, literally from *one form or condition to another*. Spiritually, in Christ, we are being changed into His likeness from one degree of glory to another with *"ever increasing glory"* (2 Cor. 3:18, Rom. 12:2, Matt. 17:2, Mark 9:2). From this same root word we get "metamorphosis." We most commonly think of metamorphosis in relation to the transformation process of a butterfly, which is an amazing parabolic picture of God's transformation for our lives.

The transformation of communities goes beyond church growth strategies, evangelistic initiatives, or a church-centered revival. Although rapid and substantial church growth and evangelism are an important part of corporate community transformation, they do not fully define transformation. George Otis, Jr. remarks: "For the term transformation to be properly applied to a community, change must be evident not only in the lives of its inhabitants, but also in the fabric of its institutions. In the end, it is dramatic social, political, and even ecological renewal that sets these cases apart from common experience."[2]

This doesn't mean that a transformed community becomes a perfect community, any more than a revived church is a perfect church. But perfection is not the measure of transformation. A transformed community may not perfect but neither can it be mistaken for its former condition. Transformation is much like sanctification: it is both an event and a process. Communities that have been impacted by God's presence and power should be measured not by what they still lack but by what they once were.[3]

After traveling the globe documenting transformed communities and closely examining over 900 case studies, George Otis Jr., defines community transformation as:

> A neighborhood, town, city or nation whose values and institutions have been overrun by the grace and presence of God. It is a place where divine fire has not merely been summoned, it has fallen. It is a culture that has been impacted by the full measure of the Kingdom of God [before future eschatological fullness]. A society in which supernatural power flows like a river of molten lava altering everything and everyone in its path. [4]

Supernatural Versus Natural Transformation

While the word "transformation" has many applications, there are basically two primary distinctions when it comes to community transformation: supernatural transformation and natural transformation.

There is a distinct difference between a reformed society and a supernaturally transformed community. Transformation is not social, political, or religious reform. Transformation is not synonymous with evangelism; evangelism is the fruit

of revival, not the means to create revival. We must not con-
fuse evangelistic strategies with hosting God's presence unto
transforming revival.

It is not possible to have *supernatural transformation* of a
community without believers first experiencing *authentic revival from heaven*. Transforming revival is a corporate revival
that brings supernatural impact on a community because of
the *manifest presence* of a *supernatural God*. Though we may be
willing partners in this process, God must be the author of
it. Since God is the author of transforming revival, it will be
characterized by both His supernatural presence and the supernatural fruit of His presence.

Participants in supernatural community transformation
are keenly aware that the systemic problems communities are
facing cannot be resolved with human wisdom or method-
ologies. Human strategies will never produce supernatural
change. Man's solutions are temporary at best and usually
flawed.

Man's resources are limited and insufficient in themselves
to solve the desperate needs of people and their communities.
Our resources only become sufficient when they are submitted to our supernatural God who is infinite and unlimited.
God has provided a redemptive answer that goes to the root
of the issues and brings comprehensive change for communities through His presence and glory.

Ministry in the Western world usually reflects a natural
(not supernatural) transformational approach. Natural or
man-based transformation is a process that man can manage
or control. People assess the desperate needs of communities,
then take an inventory of available resources, and finally allo-
cate those finite resources to address the needs. Some change
or improvement may result from the natural approach, but it
will only be a *temporary solution* for a *limited number* of people.

We face the constant reality that man-based transformation

is never enough. It is simply scratching the surface as the needs in our communities continue to multiply and spiral out of control because of sin.

Man's best intentions, sacrifice, and resources are simply not sufficient to meet the needs communities are facing today. While it is commendable to alleviate some suffering where possible in the natural realm, a natural approach cannot resolve the root problems which are spiritual in nature and continue to proliferate and continue to oppress our society. Pervasive conditions such as sexual immorality and perversion, domestic abuse, violence, and shedding of innocent blood, ruthless political schemes, governmental corruption, social injustice, prejudice, and racism will never be resolved through natural means.

The devastation prevalent in our communities is rooted in spiritual causes and therefore cannot be resolved by a man-centered approach. For example, if generations have offended the Lord by continuing in sins like immorality, idolatry, and shedding of innocent blood, the darkness and defilement that follows for a community cannot be remedied by a natural transformational effort.

When God transforms people, society, and land, He has higher purpose and unlimited resources to accomplish community transformation for His glory. God's mercy and supernatural ability to resolve and even reverse societal problems is infinitely greater than our ability or desire to do so.

God does not have to strive to resolve issues man cannot solve. God is able not only to provide pure water out of polluted water, He can also can bring it out of rocks as He did for Israel in the wilderness and has recently done for people in Brazil! He is able to do *"exceedingly abundantly above all we can ask or imagine"* (Eph. 3:20). His solutions are perfect and powerful!

When there is a polluted river (the main water source)

flowing through a community, there are two approaches to remedying the problem. The human approach would be to build a water-processing plant to purify the polluted water so it is usable for the people. The supernatural solution begins by identifying the root reason why the land is polluted and applying God's instructions for healing the situation. In Scripture and in hundreds of transformation testimonies, God brings healing supernaturally when the root causes are identified and dealt with.

In so doing, the Lord not only corrects the physical problem, His supernatural intervention and care results in redeeming people and land for His glory! A natural approach may bring an immediate remedy physically, but it does not deal with the spiritual issues necessary for God to redeem lives for His glory.

Biblical Scope of Transformation

The Biblical scope of transformation includes the lives of individual believers, transformation of the church (the Bride), transformation of spheres of society and the transformation of the land. The redemptive promise and purpose of God evidenced in the transformation process is not small, limited or temporary.

On a *personal level*, God transforms our lives through regeneration and the renewing of our minds. Paul speaks of the believer's entire life being transformed by the renewing of the mind through the Word and by the Holy Spirit (Rom. 12:2).

On a *family level*, God brings reconciliation and forgiveness as repentance occurs and root systems of sin are uprooted. As families return to covenant obedience with God and each other, relationships are restored, prodigals return home, and healing occurs.

On a *congregational level*, God restores first-love devotion, roots out religiosity, and replaces it with genuine spiritual life and power. When the transforming power of the gospel impacts believers collectively, it makes possible the transformation of the community spiritually, morally, and socially.

The transformation of individuals, their families, and congregations will lead to the transformation of the society, including land and ecology. The transformation of a village, community, region, or nation never begins at the corporate level. God first works in the hearts of believers. God transforms believers internally before He moves in a community externally.

Therefore, the Holy Spirit will be at work in the hidden places of believers' hearts, in their families, realigning congregations with His purposes, etc., long before transformation of the community becomes evident. Long-lasting transformation of a community never occurs separate from transformation at the personal, family, and congregational levels. God works from the inside out!

Transformation & Redemptive Fullness

In the God-directed progression of present redemption and revival history, the pace has accelerated as we move toward the ultimate culmination of this age. As we get closer to the return of Christ, we are seeing a fuller measure of transformational impact than ever before in history. This supernatural transformation is not simply of individuals being redeemed, but also involves a fuller redemption that now encompasses entire communities, all spheres of society, and even the land itself.

Why would God bring redemptive transformation even to land and the natural order *before* Christ returns? Clearly God is making a powerful statement about His Lordship over creation and His glory in all the earth. Supernatural transformation today among the nations is a also a more extensive expression of God's redemptive intention than the church has seen thus far in her history.

Twenty-first century revival is unlike any previous revival era and yet is in continuity with all that has preceded. Contemporary revival among the nations with its supernatural transformational fruit is an *eschatological sign* of the approaching fullness of redemption to be finalized when Christ returns to transform the whole earth into an arena for His glory (Hab. 2:14; Isa. 35; Isa. 65:17–18; Rev. 21:22–24). Transforming revival is therefore not a passing trend and is not something we can ignore. It is an eschatological sign that must not be ignored because it signals that the full manifestation of God's glory and the fullness of redemption is at hand.

The transformation that we are witnessing in the nations today is the *firstfruits* of the fuller transformation of people and land that will occur when Jesus returns to reign as King over the nations. At that time Jesus will reconcile all things in Himself. *"For God was pleased to have all his fullness dwell in Him [Christ], and through Him to reconcile to Himself all things, whether things on earth or things in heaven, by making peace through His blood, shed on the cross"* (Col. 1:19–20).

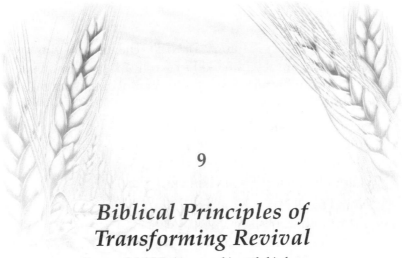

9

Biblical Principles of Transforming Revival

Forever, O LORD, Your word is settled in heaven.
Your faithfulness endures to all generations; You established the earth,
and it abides. . . . Give me understanding according to Your word.

Psalm 119:89–90, 169 NKJV

Transformation is a much overlooked biblical subject. The theme is woven like a thread through both the Old and New Testaments. The realty of transformation is pervasive in Scripture because it is an essential part of God's redemption!

If we fail to understand transformation biblically, we run the risk of treating this important reality as a passing and contemporary ministry fad. By rooting our pursuit of transforming revival in the revelation of Scripture, we are enabled to see God's redemptive picture, to understand His eternal ways, and to prepare for longterm, sustainable results.

God's Word is true and trustworthy revelation, revealing who God is in His nature, character, and intentions. God revealed His heart and nature when He assured the Jews who were going into exile for 70 years (because of their sins and the sins of their forefathers): *"For I know the plans I have for you,"* says the Lord. *"They are plans for good and not for disaster, to give you a future and a hope"* (Jer. 29:11 NLT). The journey of transformation is a journey into God's own heart and into His redemptive purposes and plans for humanity already revealed in Scripture.

We must be careful as we observe transforming revivals not only to be inspired by the transformational evidence, but also discover God and His ways. Then our hearts will seek God Himself, not just the revival He brings.

Behind God's "deeds" are always His "ways" that reveal His character and wisdom. Godly leaders in Scripture and in church history were able to lead God's people because they knew God and understood His ways. As we seek God's heart for transforming revival, like Moses, let's cry out—"make known to us Your ways, O LORD!"

A biblical principle is a basic, functional truth the essence of which is derived from Scripture, is timeless and is consistently true in all cultural contexts when implemented. A biblical principle reveals God's wisdom and ways, based on His character and nature, and is woven into the very fabric of His created order.

Because biblical principles transcend time and culture, they are a solid foundation on which to build our hope and lives in the pursuit of transforming revival. While God's transforming power may produce unique fruit in Fiji compared to Peru, all transformed communities arrive at their destination by following the very same principles from God's Word!

Whereas man-made strategies and models are not equally effective across cultural boundaries, *God's principles in Scripture transcend time, culture, ethnicity, and generations.* They work everywhere and with everybody when fully believed and followed. We must discover these same biblical principles for our own lives and communities, and trust God to lead us.

Principle #1

*God's intention in creation was to manifest
His glory and live in intimate, permanent, covenant
relationship with humankind. Man's sin and rebellion broke
that covenant bond—resulting in lost intimacy,
identity, and a defiled earth.*

The universe is designed to manifest God's glory and to reflect His eternal power and divine attributes (Job 12:7–10; Psa. 19:1–4; 50:6; 148; Rom. 1:20). Everything, whether physical or spiritual, finds its origin in God. *"He is before all things and in Him all things hold together."* Everything was created by Him and for Him so that in everything *"He might have preeminence"* (Col. 1:16-18 NKJV).

The Creator offered to Adam and Eve a perfect life of intimate fellowship with Himself and with each other, a beautiful sanctuary, meaningful responsibility to manage God's earth, and a life free from sin, sickness, disease, hatred, or any other manifestation of darkness. This relationship between God, people, and the land formed the first covenant-based spiritual bond between *God, man, and the earth.*

When Adam and Eve attempted to "be like God" by eating from the forbidden tree of the knowledge of good and evil, their disobedience broke their covenant relationship with God. Intimacy with God was broken, death began (both spiritually and physically), the land itself was defiled (cursed), the humans were expelled from the garden, hatred entered Cain's heart, and the first murder occurred.

Now in a rebellious state, humans no longer acted as royal inheritors and righteous stewards of the earth. The spirit of rebellion which entered through Adam's disobedience now infects every sphere of life. Satan has used rebellion, pride, selfishness, etc., to influence people, society, and every institution to oppose God, and to destroy people and the communities where they live. Sin against God and broken covenant with Him always has dire consequences even to this day.

Principle #2

Because humans are covenant-breakers, the framework of covenant with God must be intentionally re-established before transformation can occur.

When Adam's covenant relationship with God was fractured by sin and rebellion, the framework for relating to God and living within His covenant blessing and protection was lost. The subsequent impact of broken covenant on both people and land has been devastation.

God is a covenant-making and covenant-keeping God and requires His people to be a covenant-keeping people. As a righteous husband commits himself to exclusively love his bride and be faithful to the marriage covenant, so God seeks to relate in love and enduring (faithful) covenant. Covenant in God's eyes is an irrevocable, serious commitment that must not be broken!

God re-established a framework for a redeeming covenant relationship with humankind through the covenant He established with Abraham. God said to Abraham, *"All peoples on earth will be blessed through you"* (Gen. 12:3). In this covenant promise of God with Abraham, hope for redemption was born!

This covenant promised "a seed" through Abraham that would bring redemptive blessing to the nations of the earth (Gal. 3:14)—even Jesus Christ (Gal. 3:16). *"So those who have faith are blessed along with Abraham, the man of faith"* (Gal. 3:9).

An unmistakable biblical principle is that willful sin offends God and seriously impacts our relationship with Him and others. The only way to restore broken relationship with

God is to humble ourselves, submit to Him, confess openly our sins, and turn from our sinful ways (repentance).

Communities that are experiencing transforming revival in the twenty-first century are communities that are intentionally turning away from all known willful sin (individual and corporate sin) that offends God and breaks covenant relationship with Him (according to the standard of God's Word). These communities are intentionally preparing the way for the Lord by returning to covenant relationship with God according to His instruction in 2 Chronicles 7:14. The divine continuum of redemptive covenant from Abraham to the fullness in Jesus Christ continues today as part of the total redemptive story!

Principle #3

God has made in Jesus Christ, provision for an all-encompassing redemption through the blood of the cross for humankind and creation. Everything that was lost in the fall is now a candidate for redemptive transformation.

Transformation is necessary because everything originally created whole and life-giving is now marred and affected by sin, the evil one, and death. Creation itself experienced consequences from Adam's sin. In redemption, however, God has made every provision in Christ for re-establishing His rule and righteousness in the earth. Transformation is God redeeming and restoring people, community, and land to God's originally intended life-nurturing state. For those in redemptive covenant with God, potentially nothing is excluded from the transforming power of the cross!

Jesus instructed us to pray for His kingdom *"to come on the earth as it is in heaven."* The breadth of this revolutionary prayer includes His kingdom coming to our lives as individuals, to our families, to all spheres of society, and to defiled land—anywhere that darkness presently rules. The qualitative dimension of the Lord's Prayer—on earth *"as it is in heaven"*—means God is not interested in superficial change or temporary improvement projects! Jesus didn't die so our lives could be "improved." He died to deliver us from sin and death, to redeem us from the pit and eternal damnation, and to transform us into His image as authorized agents to further His transforming kingdom!

Transforming revival in our generation is an important manifestation of God's redemptive activity among the nations. Contemporary supernatural transformation testimonies (worldwide) provide evidence that God wants to extend redemptive transformation to people, society, and land as the *first fruit* of final redemption (Rom. 8:19).

In every arena where Satan and his kingdom have influence, we need God's manifest presence and transforming power. The devastation of people and land because of sin is humanly impossible for us to change. But it is not beyond the possibility of supernatural transformation by a redeeming God and His Son who came to earth to destroy the works of the devil and to give fullness of life (John 10:10).

Principle #4

At the core of redemption is the transformation of individuals in Christ.

The concept of transformation is profoundly biblical when understood in its spiritual and supernatural dimension. Paul uses the word "transformation" several times. He speaks of the believer's entire life being transformed by the renewing of the mind through the Word and by the Holy Spirit (Rom. 12:2). Paul's exhortation in plain English is, *"Don't copy the behavior and customs of this world, but let God transform you into a new person by changing the way you think. Then you will learn to know God's will for you, which is good and pleasing and perfect"* (Rom. 12:2 NLT).

The church in the Western world tends to preach a sweet and loving God who affirms believers in their sin and makes them comfortable in their compromise, rather than a transforming God of love who delivers believers from their sin and transforms them into the likeness of His Son. The truth-focus in the Bible is clearly on the latter!

The believer faces two possibilities: (1) being *conformed* to the spirit of the age in one's culture, or (2) being *transformed* into the image and likeness of Christ. Transformation into Christ's likeness begins with the miracle of new birth and should continue from one degree of glory to another by the Spirit through the Word and a life of intimacy with Him (2 Cor. 3:18).

God is looking for transformational *change agents* in our communities. But before He can use us to affect change in our society, He must change us so that we are *changed* agents. God leaves us in this world to carry the light and salt of the gospel as agents of hope, revival, and transformation.

The Bible clearly calls us to a theology of transformation in which our entire life is to be reconstituted in Christ for His glory and honor. The authentic Christian life is a transformational journey toward redemptive fullness. As a work in process, our transformational journey will continue until the Lord Jesus Christ returns in glory to earth, and our earthly bodies are transformed so as to be like His glorious resurrection body (Phil. 3:21).

Principle #5

Transformation of the church is a foundational principle in New Testament revelation.

Paul's theology of transformation—a theology shared by the other New Testament writers—had a corporate dimension to it. Usually the Bible speaks not in the language of individualism, but in terms of the corporate identity of God's people as the collective body of Christ. The Bible originally was written not for individuals but for the corporate, covenant people of God— whether that was Israel or the church.

Clearly God intends that transformation be a corporate reality (Eph. 2:11–13). Christ has taken two hostile groups— Gentiles and Jews—and has created them in Himself to be *"one new man"* (Eph. 2:15) and *"one body,"* reconciling *"both of them to God through the cross"* (Eph. 2:16).

Notice Paul does not focus on individual salvation but on the corporate identity of those who are being transformed— *"one body," "fellow citizens with God's people," "members of God's household,"* a *"whole building is joined together* and *rises to become a holy temple* in the Lord. . . *a [corporate] dwelling in which God lives by his Spirit"* (Eph. 2:16, 19–21).

The same process of transformation that occurs in the individual believer also happens in the corporate body of Christ as the household of faith. *"You also, like living stones, are being built into a spiritual house* [corporate] . . . .*You are a chosen people* [corporate], *a royal priesthood* [corporate], *a holy nation* [corporate], *a people belonging to God* [corporate]" (1 Pet. 2:4–5, 9).

A final image of the corporate body of Christ is the very relational and intimate image of the bride of Christ. Corporately, the bride of Christ is being transformed into the likeness of Christ and thereby being prepared to be an eternal companion for the Bridegroom.

Principle #6

Redemptive transformation in Scripture includes the possibility of community transformation.

God's nature longs to express His love, mercy, and power to people, communities, and creation in tangible and extravagant ways. Transformation is God's infinite love being tangibly expressed in a community. Transformation is possible for all communities because the Father sent His Son into the world to redeem people, and people most often live in communities. Moreover, Jesus was sent because of God's love for all humanity. "God so loved the world," includes all communities.

Devastation from sin occurs in the absence of God's manifest presence and glory. Transformation is the tangible reality of God's presence and glory among a redeemed people and their community (cf. Isa. 64:1–2, 4).

God's transforming power at work in a community will result in changing the current identity of both the church and the community spiritually, morally, and socially by beautifying them with forgiveness, cleansing, healing, deliverance, and God's manifest presence. The actual reputation of a city can change as a result of the testimony of Jesus and His living transforming power at work among the people.

A comprehensive biblical theology of transformation must include hope that encompasses communities when impacted by revival. The purpose of transforming revival and transformed communities is not only the redemption of human lives but also to manifest God's glory and bring Him *"renown, joy, praise, and honor,"* before all the nations (Jer. 33:9).

The city of Nineveh (capital of Assyria, Israel's foremost enemy) repented as a result of God's message to her through Jonah. When God forgave their sins and spared the city, Jonah complained. God said to the prophet about the city: *"Nineveh has more than a hundred and twenty thousand people who cannot tell their right hand from their left, and many cattle as well. Should I not be concerned about that great city?"* (Jonah 4:11).

God loves cities because He loves people. Community repentance is possible even for a pagan city like Nineveh because of God's mercy as Jonah witnessed. And where community repentance occurs, community transformation is likely to follow if God's presence is welcomed and comes to rest there.

Principle #7

*Redemptive transformation must be appropriated
through a process of restored covenant, repentance,
and consecration for people and communities
that revival makes possible.*

Regeneration begins with a conversion encounter with Jesus that can happen in a moment. Sanctification is the on-going process of dealing with pockets of darkness, bondage, and mindsets that need to be changed in order for us to be transformed into the likeness of Christ. This happens not only on an individual level, but can happen corporately as well when there is a corporate returning to covenant with Him.

As a redeemed people we now have authority to appropriate Christ's blood to cleanse not only our personal sin but to go back into our family and uproot sin patterns. Root systems of sin entangle families, even those who have been saved. While the blood of Jesus saves us provisionally from all sin, it is our responsibility to appropriate the work of the cross in our lives and families.

In preparing a community for transformation, the root systems of community sins that have offended God must be identified. If there is devastation and bad fruit in our community, that is evidence of a bad root system that must be identified and identificational repentance made. Daniel, himself a righteous man, fully identified with the corporate sins of his people and repented for them (see Dan. 9:3–19).

There is some compelling evidence in the Bible that indicates the transgressions of one generation may produce real consequences for future generations. For example, Jesus affirmed the notion that generational iniquities can accrue over time by pointing out that the Pharisees *"filled up"* the *"measure of the sin"* of their forefathers (Matt. 23:32–35).

God desires to break generational sin-cycles in families

and communities by identificational repentance and by releasing God's mercy on a corporate level. Nowhere is God's redeeming love more evident and extravagantly expressed than when a formerly devastated community (like Almolonga, Guatemala) becomes a presently transformed community.

For them, the desert has become a pool of water, eternal death has become eternal life, and children of wrath have become adopted children of God. God delights in taking old things and making them new, taking dead things and making them alive, taking rebellious people and turning them into lovers of God. God is a transforming God!

Principle #8

God's manifest presence is attracted to a corporate people who have abandoned themselves to prepare for His transforming presence. God's manifest presence is repelled when sin and strongholds are not dealt with by the church and community.

The *manifest presence* of God is to be distinguished from His *omni-presence.* In a real sense, God's presence is everywhere in the universe. God's manifest presence, however, is His immediate, personal, holy presence in a specific geographical area as a result of preparation that has been made for His coming.

God's manifest presence is also to be distinguished from His *indwelling presence* in the authentically regenerated believer. Although the indwelling presence of Christ by the Holy Spirit is within each blood-washed believer, the *manifest presence* of God is external to individuals and relates to His evident presence in a specific geographical location or corporate community.

That God longs to be present among His people is evident in the Bible and revival history. That God's holy presence is repelled by sin such as idolatry, sexual immorality, and innocent bloodshed is also clear in the Bible and in history. Ezekiel 8–11 describes how God withdrew His presence gradually and reluctantly from the Holy of Holies, then from the entire Temple and finally from the city because of abominable sin by His leaders and people. God's presence must be prepared for by removing every obstacle and offending sin that repels His manifest presence and holiness.

The manifest presence of God that occurs during a revival from heaven is the critical reality required to affect real redemptive change in society. When His manifest presence and glory is evident in a community, a holy awe and a holy fear of the Lord will pervade the community. And where God's presence is welcomed and received, He will dwell and rest among His redeemed ones. His resting presence will bring great blessing and transformation as when the "Ark of the Covenant" rested at Obed-Edom.

Supernatural transformation requires the presence of a supernatural God, a "demonstration of the Spirit and of power." If God's manifest presence is in the midst of His assembled people, it is safe to assume that there will be evidence and impact. In transformed communities where God's manifest presence is resting among His people, they have a presence-based faith, not just a Word-based faith.

Principle #9

The nearness of God's kingdom is available in this age. When God's kingdom comes near "on earth as it is in heaven," it will result in presence-based transformational change.

Transformation is the Holy Spirit bringing aspects of the future kingdom into the present as a down payment of full redemption. The kingdom in its fullness is yet future, coming when Jesus returns to earth at His second coming.

In the New Testament, the kingdom of God is directly related to Jesus as the Messianic King and to His mission. This fact underscores the prominence of the kingdom message in Jesus' preaching, teaching, and healing ministry (nearly 100 times in the first 3 Gospels alone).

Jesus expressed the values of God's kingdom in the Sermon on the Mount. The King and His kingdom bring presence-based transformational change. The kingdom of God is essentially a spiritual kingdom that God intends to touch every sphere of life. God's kingdom is the ultimate culture of life on planet earth. God's kingdom brings order to His creation and transformation to individuals and families, communities and regions, and even may impact nations.

Jesus instructed us to pray for God's heavenly kingdom to come to earth as part of His redemptive plan for the earth. In the Lord's Prayer (Matt. 6:10), Jesus instructed us to make declarations of faith about His kingdom. The following two phrases grammatically (in the original language) are imperatives and may be translated:

> *Kingdom of God come!*
> *Will of God be done!*
> *On earth as it is in heaven!*

When Jesus sent forth His twelve disciples, He sent them with this instruction:

> *As you go, preach this message: "The kingdom of heaven is near. Heal the sick, raise the dead, cleanse those who have leprosy, drive out demons. Freely you have received, freely give" (Matt. 10:7–8).*

Like John the Baptist and Jesus, the twelve disciples were to preach the gospel of the kingdom— i.e., the kingdom of heaven is **near** (NIV) or **at hand** (NKJV). The breaking in of God's kingdom is demonstrated when the sick are healed, the dead are raised, the lepers are cleansed, and demons are driven out of people. Transformation is the kingdom of God and the will of God in heaven being manifest on the earth.

When Jesus stepped foot in a community, things began to change! When His presence comes to a community today, things should begin to change—like transformation for broken lives, families, all spheres of society, and the land where darkness presently rules!

Such is the character of God's kingdom. As a counter-culture, it confronts the system of the world and brings redemptive change. Jesus challenged five of the seven churches in Revelation 2–3 because they had become like the culture where they lived (idolatrous and compromised) and were no longer representing the transformational power of God's kingdom.

God's kingdom is God's redemptive action in the earth that brings light to places of darkness and transformation to places of devastation. God's kingdom is not only called a kingdom of light, but also the kingdom of righteousness and the kingdom of heaven. In the midst of our wicked world, Jesus instructed us to seek first His kingdom and righteousness (Matt. 6:33)—and thus transforming revival—as a catalyst for supernatural change.

Principle #10

The culmination of great transforming revival is eschatological. Full transformation will occur when Jesus returns and brings His future kingdom to the earth.

Transforming revival is a strategic part of God's plan for bringing redemption to fullness at the end of the age. What God began in Acts 2 at Pentecost, and what He poured out globally in the outpouring of the Spirit in the twentieth century, He is now ready to bring to fullness. Current transformational miracles of land are an eschatological precursor of the approaching fullness of redemption when Christ returns to transform the whole earth into an arena for His glory (Hab. 2:14, Isa. 35; Isa. 65:17–18, Rev. 21:22–24).

Although complete redemption of the earth awaits Christ's second coming, clearly ecological miracles and supernatural transformation of land testimonies are appearing around the world as the *first fruits* of final redemption. As the church approaches the end of the age, forerunner eschatological phenomena will increase.

On the dark side, evil will reach its ultimate expression under an antichrist-world system with its own defilement of the earth. On the God side, however, the occurrence of first fruit of the fullness of redemption will increase and intensify as well. Nowhere does Scripture teach that evil triumphs and redemption diminishes during the eschatological drama of the end.

A whole world of transformation is present in the power and victory of the cross that we have hardly begun to understand or experience. An approach to Scripture like that of the Scribes in Jesus' day will overlook portions of biblical revelation that clearly describe transformation on a corporate and ecological scale.

Isaiah 35 is one of these passages. It is not simply poetic language to be spiritualized (as in most sermons). Rather, the chapter is boldly prophetic and descriptive of eschatological transformation. In Isaiah 35 the entire landscape is changing. The spiritual atmosphere is changing and even the land is being transformed.

Description of transformation in Isaiah 35 occurs at two levels—the physical and the spiritual. The *spiritual dimension* is clearly indicated when the highway is called "the Way of Holiness" and a road on which only the redeemed will walk (35:8, 9). Because the glory of God's presence is being openly manifested and glorious transformation is resulting, God's people are overtaken with joy and gladness (35:10). This is revival at its best!

The *physical dimension* of transformation of this chapter is also apparent. The core message is about the manifestation of God's glory and splendor in the earth. As a direct consequence of God's public manifestation of His glory, supernatural transformation follows. Previously cursed and barren land is transformed into a green and blooming landscape. Signs and wonders occur involving the physical transformation of the blind, the deaf, the lame, and the mute. Where before there was desolate desert inhabited by jackals, there is now life-giving water with water-loving reeds and papyrus growing. Because of the manifestation of God's splendor and glory, life springs forth everywhere.

It is noteworthy that Isaiah's preceding chapter (Isa. 34) describes God's judgment among the nations, while this chapter (Isa. 35) graphically describes God's redemption in transformational language. Isaiah's prophetic declaration in chapter 35 has several levels of fulfillment. Fulfillment begins with the first coming of Jesus Christ and reaches its fullest realization at His second coming.

In connection with His first coming, the church (as described in the Book of Acts) was a full participant in this transformational prophecy. In relation to His second coming, the church during the great end-time revival immediately preceding His coming will also be a full participant in this transformational picture. These two strategic points of redemptive history are the ultimate standard and expression of transformation.

In summary, the Bible reveals that supernatural transformation occurs at various levels—individuals, church, community, and land. These biblical principles of transformation provide a scriptural grid for understanding the global data about supernatural transformation that is now increasingly occurring among the nations. The church's present strategic location near the end of the redemptive story provides the *sitz im leben* for understanding the contemporary revival history that is unfolding in our century!

10

Extraordinary Prayer & Revival

The prayer of faith will save the sick. . . .The effective, fervent prayer of
a righteous man avails much. Elijah. . . prayed earnestly. . . . And he
prayed again, and the heavens gave rain.

James 5:15–18 (NKJV)

God's redemptive purposes *on the earth* are always
birthed through extraordinary prayer. Likewise, the
purpose of God *in revival* is always birthed through extraordinary prayer! God uses the *corporate* intercession of humble and
obedient people as His appointed means for cutting a channel from heaven to earth. Through the corporate agreement in
prayer, He pours out His Spirit in revival for the church and
in spiritual awakening for the community.

When intercession for revival is corporate, individual
prayer increases greatly in effectiveness—not by addition, but
by multiplication. This is the principle of synergism: the combined effect of corporate prayer is greater than the sum of all
the individual parts.

Extraordinary prayer for revival is not primarily heroic
individual intercessory efforts. Rather, extraordinary intercession for revival is intentional and united prayer by leaders
and people of all denominations who are willing to intercede
together for the sake of revival and salvation in their city.

United, corporate intercession is not optional; it is absolutely necessary for revival from heaven to occur. Dr. A. T. Pearson once said: "There has never been a spiritual awakening in any country or locality that did not begin with united prayer."[1]

Andrew Murray, a great intercessor in South Africa who helped pray in a revival in his nation, said concerning the power of united prayer: "God rules the world by the prayers of His saints, that prayer is the power by which Satan is conquered; that by prayer the Church on earth has disposal of the powers of the heavenly world."[2]

God gives His kingdom authority in prayer only to those who are walking humbly and living in covenant with Him and with other believers. The historical precedent of united, corporate intercession as a necessary component for the occurrence of great revival is a consistent pattern.

History-Shaping Prayer

In the **Eighteenth-Century English Revival,** George Whitefield and John Wesley, joined about 60 Moravians in a corporate prayer meeting in London on New Year's Eve, 1738. As they continued in earnest and focused prayer for revival, the Holy Spirit broke in upon them (as at Pentecost) around 3 A.M. This marked the first observable beginning of the great English awakening that started in 1739 and lasted until the death of John Wesley in 1791.[3] Such power in united prayer for revival is extraordinary!

At the beginning of the **eighteenth century, Count Zinzendorf**, a Lutheran, was crying out to God for revival. As a result, the Moravian community was birthed as a praying community with an unbroken chain of intercession for 100 years. That is extraordinary prayer!

At the beginning of the nineteenth century, when John

Wesley died, God's people began crying out for another great awakening and God answered from heaven with the Second Great Awakening on two continents. That is extraordinary prayer!

In the mid-nineteenth century, at the **New York City Prayer Meeting Revival**, Jeremiah Lamphier started a Wednesday noonday prayer meeting for businessmen in the Dutch Reformed Church in lower Manhattan. The first week (September 23, 1857) only 6 people showed up out of a population of one million. The next time there were 14; the third time 23 men joined him. This humble beginning illustrates how God starts every great revival with the corporate prayer of his people.

God so breathed on the New York City prayer meetings until (by February of 1858) prayer was occurring every noonday in every church and every public building downtown. This revival then spread through New England and the nation. Church bells would bring people to pray at 8:00 A.M., 12 noon, and 6:00 P.M. J. Edwin Orr's research reveals that in 1858–59 one million Americans were converted in a population of thirty million and at least a million Christians also were renewed, with lasting results in church attendances and moral reform to society.[4]

Ministers in Atlantic City, New Jersey, reported during the Prayer Meeting Revival only 50 adults remained unconverted, out of a population of 50,000. In Portland, Oregon, 240 department stores would close daily from 11 A.M. to 2 P.M. for prayer. They signed an agreement among themselves so that no one would cheat and stay open.

This revival then jumped the Atlantic and broke out in Northern Ireland, Scotland, Wales, England, South Africa, South India, and everywhere people were united in praying for revival. The revival's effect was felt for 40 years. The revival began as a corporate prayer meeting, and it was sustained by a movement of prayer.

At the turn of the **twentieth century**, there was need again of spiritual awakening, and Christians began praying all around the world for revival. What followed this great groundswell of corporate prayer for revival were two revivals of enormous outcome in the first decade of the twentiety century—(1) the British Welsh Revival of 1904–06; and (2) the Los Angeles Azusa Street Revival of 1906–09.

There were prayer meetings at Moody Bible Institute in Chicago, the Keswick Convention in England, in Melbourne (Australia), in India, in Korea—all around the world people were praying that God would send another great revival and spiritual awakening in the twentieth century. In 1904, the Welsh revival began and spread far and wide among the nations. Prayer— extraordinary prayer—made that possible!

The worldwide corporate prayer by God's people for revival was answered by God from heaven with worldwide results. The Welsh and Azusa Street revivals were the first revivals ever to go global in their spread, influence, and impact. In the aftermath of this fire from heaven, revival fire was carried or ignited in nations on every continent as well as many islands of the sea like Indonesia.

This prayer pattern continues **in the twenty-first century.** Corporate prayer for revival is exploding throughout the nations. Contemporary corporate intercession for revival is every bit as remarkable as the examples mentioned from history and even more so! This unprecedented prayer is contending for the unprecedented end-time revival and harvest that is coming. Only extraordinary prayer will birth the extraordinary redemptive plans of God at the end of the age!

What is Extraordinary Prayer?

Jonathan Edwards wrote a book called, *A Humble Attempt to Promote Explicit Agreement and Visible Union of God's People in Extraordinary Prayer for the Revival of Religion and the Extension of Christ's Kingdom on Earth.* When Jonathan Edwards mentions "extraordinary prayer" in this long book title, what did he have in mind? What is extraordinary prayer for revival?

When people give up their lunch time to join others in praying for revival, that is extraordinary prayer! When people rise early in the morning to go to a 4 A.M. prayer meeting to cry out for God's manifest presence, that is extraordinary prayer!

When *Hannah* cried out to God in agonizing prayer for a son (1 Sam. 1:7–18), God heard her prayer. That is extraordinary prayer! So extraordinary was Hannah's prayer that as a result she conceived Samuel the prophet and thus birthed the old covenant prophetic movement.

When *Elijah* prayed on Mt. Carmel (1 Kgs. 18:36–38), the fire of God fell from heaven. That is extraordinary prayer! Then Elijah prayed again and again (7 times) until the skies yielded rain from heaven, thereby ending God's judgment on Israel of the 3½ year-drought. That is extraordinary prayer!

When *Daniel* (see Dan. 9:1–23) interceded for Israel's restoration according to God's promise (through Jeremiah) about "after seventy years," Daniel's prayer made possible the release of the Jews from Babylonian/Persian captivity so they could return to their homeland. That is extraordinary prayer!

Concerning the prayers of the righteous, Peter Kreeft states:

> I strongly suspect that if we saw all the difference even the tiniest of our prayers to God make, and all the people those little prayers were destined to affect, and all the consequences of those effects down through the centuries, we would be so paralyzed with awe at the power of prayer that we would be unable to get up off our knees for the rest of our lives.[5]

This stunning quote does not apply to all prayer, however.

All prayers clearly are not created equal. If all prayers were equal, they would all have the same effect. On the contrary, there are two kinds of effects that prayers can have. Some prayers avail nothing; other prayers avail much! What makes the difference?

Prayers that avail nothing comes only from the head and does not engage the heart. These are the prayers of religious duty. Religious prayers from a cold or lukewarm heart avail nothing! They have no effect! The Bible indicates that prayers prayed while willfully sinning avail nothing: *"Your iniquities have separated you from your God; your sins have hidden his face from you, so that he will not hear"* (Isa. 59:2).

Prayers that avail much are prayers of faith, earnest prayers, the prayers of the righteous and persevering prayers. This kind of praying is extraordinarily effective! Prayers that arise from a broken and contrite heart may not sound pretty, but they are prayers that will be heard in the courts of heaven and in the end avail much. *"He will fulfill the desire of those who fear Him; He also will hear their cry and save them"* (Psa. 145:19 NKJV). Obviously extraordinary prayer for revival is prayer of this kind.

Covenant Prayer

Praying from within covenant relationship with God is extraordinary prayer. God says, *"Call upon Me and come and pray to Me and I will listen to you"* (Jer. 29:12 NAS). This is a covenant promise by God to His people. Revival breakthroughs come when God's people, who are desperate for His manifest presence, take seriously His covenant promises by earnestly seeking Him in prayer and fasting, with faith and repentance.

God says there are two things that He exalts and honors above all else: His Name and His Word (Psa. 138:2, NIV). God not only blesses those who read, study, and meditate on His Word, He also blesses those who sing and pray His Word back to Him.

A vivid example of covenant prayer occurred in the Hebrides Revival. A core of God-hungry believers began to pray about God's covenant promises. They appealed to God from Scriptures like Isaiah 44:3 where God says: *"For I will pour water on him who is thirsty, And floods on the dry ground; I will pour My Spirit on your descendants, And my blessing on your offspring . . . "* (NKJV).

Intercessors in the Hebrides took seriously God's Word in 2 Chronicles 7:14–15 and prayed earnestly according to God's instruction and conditions in this covenant promise. They believed God was a covenant-keeping God and would let none of His covenant promises fall to the ground. As they prayed, God spoke to them about heart issues through Psalm 24. They responded to God by crying out for *"clean hands and a pure heart"* (24:4a) and for lives free from any taint of idolatry or deceitfulness.

As earnest believers in the Hebrides prayed the Scriptures and humbly submitted to God's authority, the fire of God's Word and Spirit mingled together as light and life-giving revelation in their hearts and in their prayers. They prayed with holy passion! They prayed with humble and repentant hearts! They prayed God's covenant promises! And God answered from heaven with an extraordinary revival with community transformation. The Hebrides revival reveals the importance of extraordinary prayer that precedes God's visitation from heaven.[6]

Effective prayer is covenant-praying. Covenant-praying is living in covenant relationship with God and taking God's Word and promises seriously as covenant agreements. Many of God's promises are conditional as in 2 Chronicles 7:14. God says, *"If My people will... then I will."*

The covenant promises of God provide a clear basis for faith and obedience. It provides ground for being persistent and tenacious in both prayer and faith, not giving up when there is no immediate answer. Living in covenant with God has always been the key by which men and women of faith have contended at the throne before God with results happening on the earth.

Instruction in 2 Chronicles 7:14

The foundational strategy that undergirds all great revivals in history is God's instruction and timeless principles in 2 Chronicles 7:14. This Scripture is a clear direction of returning to covenant relationship with the Lord. As such, this passage of scripture—above all others—has been the divine "prescription" followed by God's covenant people in all great revivals (including contemporary transforming revivals) when preparing for God's visitation.

God's instruction in 2 Chronicles 7:13–14 (NKJV) is:

> *"When I shut up heaven . . . , if My people who are called by My name will humble themselves, and pray and seek My face, and turn from their wicked ways, then I will hear from heaven, and will forgive their sin and heal their land.*

Notice God Himself closes the heavens (physically or spiritually). He then gives a conditional covenant promise: *If my people will, then I will.* God promises to do His part if God's people (corporately) are willing to do their part. The part that God requires from His people (who are called by His name) is embodied in a *fourfold instruction:*

> "humble themselves,
>> and pray
>>> and seek My face,
>>>> and turn from their wicked ways."

The part that God will do when His people have done their part is stated clearly in His *threefold promise:*

> "I will hear from heaven
> And will forgive their sin
> And heal their land."

This covenant promise with its timeless principles couldn't be plainer. But some object that this is an old covenant promise to Israel and no longer applies under the new covenant. This objection breaks down in several ways:

(1) It overlooks the *spiritual continuity* between the Abrahamic, Mosaic, and Davidic covenants with the new covenant (Gal. 3:6–9, 29).

(2) The *spiritual principles* in 2 Chronicles 7:13–14 relate to God's nature and ways, and are therefore timeless principles. This is who God is, what He is like and how He relates to His people corporately whether in a community, region or nation.

(3) The objection ignores astonishing *contemporary evidence* that God still relates to His covenant people (whether Jew or Gentile) corporately according to His instruction and spiritual principles stated in 2 Chronicles 7:14—even to the point of healing the physical land in numerous places (Almolonga and Fiji being examples) when His instruction is followed wholeheartedly and corporately.

The great twentieth century outpouring of the Holy Spirit at Azusa Street that went around the world was built on the foundation of 2 Chronicles 7:14. Likewise the Hebrides Revival in the mid twentieth century was ignited by the extraordinary prayer of humble people who took God's covenant instruction in 2 Chronicles 7:14 seriously. This promise and its instruction is to be obeyed, not just prayed about.

Around the world in the twenty-first century, wherever transforming revival is producing the fruit of transformed communities, these communities all have one thing in common—namely, from the outset they all seriously followed God's instruction in 2 Chronicles 7:14. And they all engage in extraordinary prayer for revival.

Humble Prayer

Matthew Henry once remarked: "When God intends great mercy for his people, the first thing he does is to set them a praying." Serious prayer for God's intervention first involves humbling ourselves before Him (often with fasting). Humility must be our heart's posture as we come in prayer to seek God's face and favor.

Humility is lowliness of mind, yieldedness to God, freedom from self exaltation and self promotion, freedom from vanity and pride, and a meekness that "expresses a spirit of willingness and obedience and a lack of resistance to God's dealings with us."[7]

The Hebrew word for "humble" means "to be bowed down"; particularly it means to be bowed down before God. Humility is first and foremost toward God (Matt. 11:29; Jas. 1:21). Humility is a childlike bowing before God and His Word.

2 Chronicles 7:14 says: *"If my people . . . . will humble themselves."* This is a big "if." The first step in God's instruction is the step of humility. The church typically jumps over this first step and just begins to pray, seek God's face and repent of this and that. But the step of humility must not be passed over!

Jesus repeatedly took that first step of humility! The eternal Son of God humbled Himself greatly in the incarnation. Likewise, Jesus humbled Himself greatly at the cross and voluntarily submitted to our sins' punishment and God's wrath. Jesus humbled himself again and again! We too must take the first step of humility if we are to fully know God's presence and encounter His glory.

Some people believe that sinning is what will keep us humble. Others believe that self-condemnation is the secret of humility. On the contrary, it is the grace of God that leads us out of the pit of self preoccupation and sinfulness to the place of knowing God in His glory as Creator and His love as Redeemer. It is this grace that makes humility possible.

In the spirit of 2 Chronicles 7:14, to humble ourselves is to admit our need and spiritual drought; and to pray is to reconnect our hearts to God in a real and honest way. Humble praying is selfless praying, prayer that focuses not on what we want but on God and His glory.

Humble praying is a willingness to lay one's life down for the sake of God's glory. Moses and Paul wanted to see the salvation of their people so much that they were willing even to be blotted out of God's book (Exod. 32:32; Rom. 9:3). This kind of prayer says, *"Not unto us, O LORD, not unto us, but to Your name give glory, because of Your mercy, because of Your truth."* (Psa. 115:1 NKJV).

So much of our prayers are self-serving and self-centered. Humble praying is being so united with God in prayer that it truly is His heart and His purpose that is being sought. This kind of prayer takes hold of the promises of God and pulls them into present fulfillment. This is extraordinary prayer for revival!

David Brainerd, whose diary was carefully edited by Jonathan Edwards, humbly devoted his young adult life interceding for the salvation of the Native Americans in Massachusetts. Look at his *humble tenacity* as he coughs up blood in the New England snow while interceding for revival among the Indians. Shortly before he died at age 29, he saw the answer to his prayer as revival broke out among the Indians to whom Brainerd had been ministering. That is extraordinary prayer!

Prayer that Seeks God's Face

2 Chronicles 7:14 contains a timeless principle from God: *If my people . . . will humble themselves and pray and **seek My face** . . , then I will hear from heaven.* God highlights this same timeless principle when He speaks through Jeremiah: *Then you will call upon me and come and pray to me, and I will listen to you. You will seek me and find me when you seek me with all your heart* (Jer. 29:12–13).

Seeking God's face is an important part of renewing covenant with God. One's face represents the essence of who a person is. To see a person's face is to see that person. Thus, seeking God's face is drawing close to Him personally and intimately. Seeking Him with all our heart is an undistracted pursuit, giving Him our full attention. It is joining the Psalmist in resolute pursuit: *"Your face, LORD, I will seek"* (Psa. 27:8).

God says that when we seek Him with all our heart (with our full attention), He will be found by us. God never said "seek Me and it will be in vain." That is the lie of Satan that will come to us when we resolve to seek Him with all of our heart. Seeking Him will never be for nothing! God reassures us that if we will seek Him, He will be found and His kingdom will advance (cf., Heb. 11:6).

When David became Israel's king, He gave his heart and attention to bringing the Ark of the Covenant [i.e., the presence of God] to Jerusalem. In the midst of rejoicing when the ark returned, David made this passionate plea: *"Seek the Lord and His strength; Seek His face continually"* (1 Chron. 16:11 NASB). David knew the principle of seeking the Lord with all his heart.

Often we give the Lord token time and attention, the kind of attention that would be an insult to someone we love. David understood that to know God, we have to give Him time and attention from our heart, not just token duty or obedience. God wants intimacy with His people. He is overjoyed when His people seek His face with undistracted devotion.

Seeking God requires focus! Distractions abound when we resolve to contend for the priority of praying for revival in our daily schedule. We cannot escape the fact that life in the twenty-first century is way too fast-paced. We are no longer just busy but feverishly busy; we are no longer just in a hurry but have hectic schedules with little time for God. This has personal consequences and repercussions for our families and congregations.

One of the first things to suffer in a busy schedule is one's prayer life. To seek God earnestly as our highest priority requires *fasting and prayer* on a regular basis. In Joel 2:15–16 everyone in the congregation of Israel without exception was called to participate in a fast before the Lord.

The word "fast" means to voluntarily deny oneself food, or other daily activities for the purpose of seeking God's face.

Here are three ways we can fast in order to seek God's face.

(1) *Fasting food:* Fasting from food helps bring our flesh into submission to the Spirit. Many Western believers (like their culture) are obsessed with food—rich foods, big meals, snacks, candy, pastries, desserts, fast-foods, caffeine drinks, etc. Fasting for spiritual purposes serves notice on our physical appetite by saying, "You are my servant, not my master."

Fasting from food is a way we can set our heart wholeheartedly on seeking the Lord. Fasting helps clarify our motives, purify our hearts, and gives us energy to seek God's face. It enables us to hear God more clearly and to receive from Him more fully. Fasting food is one of God's appointed means for spiritual and physical cleansing.

(2) *Fasting media:* Fasting from the media has the benefit of

clearing our spiritual environment from all distraction and defilement that comes through visual media like television, cinema, DVDs and the internet. Try seeking the Lord with all your heart by eliminating the media for a period of time to concentrate and focus entirely on seeking God's face.

(3) *Fasting conversation:* Fasting from having conversations is one of the best ways to quiet our hearts before God. Fasting from our cell phone (or texting) helps to quiet our spirit and to focus on Him. The discipline of silence is one of the most needed spiritual disciplines in our culture. Limiting the amount of talking will enable our words to be more meaningful when we do speak. James says, *"Everyone should be quick to listen, **slow to speak**, and slow to become angry"* (Jas. 1:19 emphasis added).

When seeking God's face with prayer and fasting, whether individually or corporately, the enemy will resist. We must know that our flesh is at war with our spirit, and our spirit must resist the flesh's objections. Don't be overwhelmed or surprised by the reaction of your flesh or the attempts of the enemy to keep you in the status quo of your life. Follow the instruction of James in 4:7–8: *Submit yourselves then to God. Resist the devil, and he will flee from you. Come near to God and he will come near to you.*

Recognize the attempt of the enemy to make you back off fasting, because He knows what an important component this is in seeking God's face and finding Him. It will require *a step of faith* to move from where you are to a renewed pursuit of God's face for, *"without faith it is impossible to please God"* (Heb. 11:6). The motivation for our faith is the assurance, *"he rewards those who earnestly seek him"* (Heb. 11:6c).

Unrelenting Prayer

Most Christians, who take prayer seriously, pray fervently in fits and starts. Unrelenting intercession is important for breakthroughs in revival. Earnest prayer is the prayer that lays hold of God and won't let go. It is the prayer that allows Him to break us and to mold us into the likeness and character of Jesus.

God says the unrelenting, earnest prayer of righteous men avails much (Jas. 5:16). Alferd Lord Tennyson, the great British poet, said in his day:

> More things are wrought by prayer
> Than this world dreams of.

The truth of James 5:16 and Tennyson's statement is evident all through the Bible and all through history.

- Joshua prayed, the sun stood still and a great victory was won for Israel.
- Elijah prayed and the fire of God fell from heaven.
- Daniel prayed and the mouths of lions were closed.
- Jesus prayed, "Not My will but Yours be done," and gave the world the power of the cross.
- The Moravians prayed for over 100 years and modern missions was born.
- John Wesley prayed and revival came to England that spared her the devastation of the French Revolution.
- Believers prayed in Almolonga, Guatemala, and a city was saved and the land healed.

Earnest, righteous, faith-filled prayer truly avails much! It always has and it always will. When such prayer moves from individual praying to corporate intercession, the effectiveness of prayer increases exponentially. Such prayer moves angels in heaven to accomplish the agenda of God on the earth.

Spiritual awakening and community transformation are always born from the womb of intercession. The weakness of our confidence in the effectiveness of prayer is seen in how little time and energy we put into prayer, versus how much time and energy we put into our own weak human initiatives to make things happen.

It is eternally important that we focus on moving heaven through earnest intercession whereby God, Himself responds and angels are dispatched to bring about change, rather than trying to move earth and make things happen on our own.

Mention of the incense (prayers) of the saints in Revelation (Rev. 5:8; 8:3–4), indicates that the intercessory prayers of believers are extremely important in the ultimate destruction of evil and the establishment of righteousness on the earth. God in some sense collects (in heaven) the prayers of the righteous and stores them up for strategic moments in history.

Although God may not answer all our prayers immediately, He does not throw them aside; rather, He collects and keeps them for the strategic time of their fulfillment. Unrelenting prayer is extraordinary prayer from God's point of view.

The small Moravian community in east Germany experienced an outpouring of the Holy Spirit in 1727. They then began a 24-hour unbroken chain of prayer for the spread of revival and the gospel to the nations. That chain of prayer continued unbroken for 100-plus years. That is extraordinary, unrelenting prayer!

Desperate Prayer

One of the fundamental differences between the non-Western church and the Western church is the level of desperation in the lives of God's people. Affluence in the Western world numbs the appetite for God's presence and gives the church a false sense of security. Desperation is the underlying fuel that ignites our hearts and enables us to engage in extraordinary prayer for revival.

Holy desperation for God's manifest presence and Jesus' ministry is required for us to move out of our complacent, satisfied existence. Everything else must be secondary to this consuming desire. In communities where transforming revival is occurring, the people of God are desperate enough to change their lifestyle, their priorities, their time, and resource commitments and to make everything else a secondary activity to their desperate pursuit of God in their midst. They "cry out" in desperation and the Lord heard their cry.

In the Western world we may agree that revival is desirable, but where is the cry of desperation that pierces through religious rhetoric and awakens the human heart to seek God. Look at the world around us, watch the news, take a good look at your city. We are a people in desperate need of revival from heaven.

The Bible makes a distinction between "prayer" and "calling aloud" or "crying out" to God. In Jeremiah 33:3 God said to those in captivity, *"Call to Me and I will answer you."* The word "call" in Hebrew is *qara* which carries the meaning of "calling aloud" or "crying out in desperation."

In our impossible circumstances which we cannot change with our own resources, our crying out to God is a humbling reminder of our total inability to bring about real change apart from God's intervention. God promises that if we will call aloud or cry out to Him, He will listen (Jer. 29:12).

Not only will He listen, He promises to answer us from heaven (Jer. 33:3). God's response from heaven includes revelation—*"I will show you great and mighty things you do not know"* (Jer. 33:3), as well as supernatural power to deliver and to accomplish His redemptive purpose in our city.

The context of the Jeremiah's 33:3 promise is the transformation of the city. God promises:

> *"I will bring health and healing to it (Jer. 33:6)."*
>
> *"I will cleanse them from all the sin they have committed against me and will forgive all their sins of rebellion (Jer, 33:8)."*
>
> *"Then,"* God declares, *"this city will bring me renown, joy, praise and honor before all nations on earth that hear of all the good things I do for it; and they will be in awe and tremble at the abundant prosperity and peace I provide for it (Jer 33:9)."*

Are you, or family members, or your community in a hopeless situation. Call to Him, cry out to Him for deliverance! Don't be passive—call out to God, cry out in desperation to Him for deliverance! Desperate prayer is extraordinary prayer!

Thailand's Desperate Prayer

The revival that is taking place in the Omkoi Province of Thailand is being fueled by prayer and fasting. For over ten years much prayer has gone up for revival in the tribal areas of northern Thailand. Before a key conference in 2007, the Karen tribe was mobilized to pray and fast, and they did—more than 10,000 days cumulatively. The Lord used that conference to encourage believers to pray, fast, and seek God for a similar movement of God in Omkoi.

By January 2007, the Spirit of God was powerfully answering their prayers. In village after village, the Spirit of God was touching hearts. In many cases, this movement was being led by the children. Children, sometimes as young as four years old, would be worshipping, and in some cases seeing visions of heaven, hell, and the crucifixion of Jesus.

In March 2007, at a Karen camp in Omkoi with ten thousand people, there was a powerful move of repentance for sins committed between the Karen and the Northern Thais. As a result, the revival has now spread to the whole region. In Omkoi, nearly half of the 200 villages now have a church. In a country where the Christian population is only 0.3%, in Northern Thailand that percentage is now about 2.88%. Secular TV declared "Karen tribe is first Christian community in Thailand".

Many villages that have now gone through the "Healing the Land" transformation process and have seen miraculous healing of their land. Since 2007, they have seen an increase in crops. In one case, a family which has usually harvested only about 10 sacks of rice a season is now harvesting 100. In areas of newly-planted rice crops, the harvest was four times what would have been the normal yield. In addition both the size and the quantity of fish have increased, and villages where there was insufficient water now have an abundant supply.

Leaders report the reason for this amazing touch of transformation in Northern Thailand is their pursuit of prayer, fasting, repentance, and reconciliation. In 2006, the goal was to have a composite total of 10,000 days of prayer and fasting for transformation. In 2009, their goal had increased to 100,000 days of fasting and prayer. God is indeed answering their prayers! [8]

Priestly Prayer

George Whitefield read and prayed the Bible through on his knees many times as he would intercede for the salvation of the thousands to whom he was preaching. That is extraordinary priestly intercession!

A man named "Brother Nash" travelled ahead of Charles Finney to intercede for revival of the people in the location where Finney was scheduled to preach. Nash was never a public man, but served instead as an unselfish intercessor behind the scenes of Finney's revival ministry. Often Nash was on his face before God in prayer underneath the platform (or back room) while Finney preached. That is extraordinary priestly prayer!

All believers have the privilege and responsibility to be mediators before God on behalf of their neighbors, community, and nation. We actually partner with the intercession of Jesus by agreeing with His heart and His mind for the salvation of the lost.

Ezekiel, at the time of Judah's spiritual, moral, and political corruption, recorded God's call for the righteous to intercede for their city and nation:

> *I sought for a man among them who would make a wall, and stand in the gap before Me on behalf of the land, that I should not destroy it; but I found no one. Therefore I have poured out My indignation on them; I have consumed them with the fire of My wrath; and I have recompensed their deeds on their own heads," says the Lord GOD* (Ezek. 22:30–31 NKJV).

God is again calling for intercessors to take their place as "watchmen" on the walls of their cities, praying day and night, taking the responsibility for their cities, reminding God of His Word and covenant promises and "[giving] *Him no rest until He establishes [our cities] a praise on the earth*" (Isa. 62:7). Intercessory watchmen stir God's heart to have mercy and spare the city.

Every person who is born-again and part of God's family is a member of "the royal priesthood" and "chosen generation" (1 Pet. 2:9). This isn't a special calling for a few; this is part of our identity as the Bride of Christ. We can approach the throne of God with confidence in prayer because of Jesus' shed blood as "the worthy Lamb."

To be a watchman is to "watch," be alert, vigilant, and awake. In ancient times, watchmen were those who stood guard on the protective walls of the city and communicated with the guards of the gates. To "watch" in the spiritual sense is the same. We as a "royal priesthood" are given the privilege and responsibility to watch over our cities through prayer.

> *I have set watchmen on your walls, O Jerusalem; they shall never hold their peace day or night. You who make mention of the LORD, do not keep silent, and give Him no rest till He establishes and till He makes Jerusalem a praise in the earth* (Isa. 62:6–7 NKJV)

Intercessors, put your priestly garments back on! When the corporate church begins to intercede on behalf of the city, a grace "canopy" (made possible by prayer) begins to cover the city. That means it is possible for the church in a local region to begin to pray in agreement for God's kingdom to come down on the earth as it is in heaven. When the united, corporate prayer of agreement happens, heaven begins to touch and influence the earth.[9]

Human strategies don't bring revival; revival comes when God answers by fire from heaven. Fire from God's throne doesn't fall without sacrifices; fire doesn't fall on empty altars. God waits to send His fire until the sacrifice is prepared and laid on the altar. God waits to send fire from His throne until the priestly intercessors are standing in the gap on behalf of the perishing.[10]

Conclusion

The goal is for God's kingdom to come and *His will to be done* in our part of the earth as it done in heaven. God has a salvation "will" for your city; it is already in His heart. Priestly prayer intercedes for God's kingdom and will to become a reality in our neighborhood and community.

If we are willing "to prepare the way" for the Lord's visitation with extraordinary prayer, then God will partner with us. Extraordinary revival must be preceded by extraordinary prayer!

> *And the [intercessory] fire on the altar shall be kept burning on it; it shall not be put out. And the priest shall burn wood on it every morning. . . . A fire [of intercession] shall always be burning on the altar; it shall never go out* (Lev. 6:1213 NKJV).

When believers begin to cry out to the Lord corporately and continually like the Moravians, that is truly extraordinary prayer! God is raising the bar of unrelenting, united, priestly, corporate intercession for a global revival and a massive end-time harvest.

11

The Fire of Repentance & Revival

Repent therefore, and turn again, that your sins may be blotted out, that times of refreshing may come from the presence of the Lord,

Acts 3:19–20, ESV

Historically, repentance is part of the preparation that precedes and accompanies great revival visitations. It is part of the housecleaning that prepares for the heavenly visitor. Paul writes: *Do you not know "that the kindness of God ("goodness of God" NKJV) leads you to repentance?* (Rom. 2:4, NASB). Corporate repentance, especially, often signals the beginning of God's goodness and manifest presence drawing near in revival.

Repentance is not something that happens only at conversion; repentance is an on-going necessity in our life in order for us to remain clean and connected in our hearts with God. When we let even small or inadvertent sins accumulate in our lives without repentance, it leads to spiritual defilement, dullness, and even a relational disconnect from God.

Just as repentance is necessary for individuals to have a healthy relationship with God and to experience spiritual transformation, so it is necessary corporately for the body of Christ to experience times of spiritual refreshing, revival, and transformation.

Revival of Repentance

When John the Baptist's revival began, it was clearly a revival of repentance. The people began to catch the wind of the Spirit, the voice of the Lord thundered in John's message, and a revival of repentance broke out in Judea and spread throughout Israel and beyond.

During John's ministry, the people came from great distances and publicly confessed their sin and were baptized for sin's remission and cleansing. It says that John the Baptist came in the spirit and power of Elijah to turn the hearts of the fathers to their children and the children's hearts back to their fathers.

Mark 1:9 testifies that "at that time" Jesus came and was baptized, and thereby openly identified with this revival of repentance. Jesus is always attracted to and identifies with the people who will humble themselves, earnestly seek Him, and turn from their wicked ways. He is drawn like a magnet to people and places who sincerely repent (as we see throughout revival history).

Repentance is a key to God's restored favor and presence. Until we are willing to face the probing by the Holy Spirit of our own hearts, a revival of repentance will not happen on a larger scale.

> *"Even now," declares the LORD, "return to me with all your heart, with fasting and weeping and mourning."* **Rend your heart** *and not your garments.* **Return to the LORD** *your God, for he is gracious and compassionate, slow to anger and abounding in love, and he relents from sending calamity. Who knows? He may turn and have pity and leave behind a blessing* (Joel 2:12–14a, emphasis added).

Corporate confession of sin is often the flash point at which great revival fire is ignited. This was true of the great Moravian revival in 1727, the Hebrides Revival in 1949, and many college revivals—as recent as Asbury College (1970) and Wheaton College (1995). All these, like the John the Baptist revival, were preeminently revivals of repentance.

God makes clear in Proverbs 28:13 that *"He who conceals his sins does not prosper, but whoever confesses and renounces them finds mercy."* Daniel understood this spiritual law: *"All this disaster has come upon us, yet we have not sought the favor of the LORD our God by turning from our sins and giving attention to your truth"* (Dan. 9:13).

It is time for a major revival of repentance in the Western world; and that revival must begin in the churches. The church needs to repent for being more interested in her own success and how she appears externally before men, than she is about the foremost issues of God's kingdom and what He thinks about the condition of our communities.

Is Repentance Necessary?

The message of repentance is not popular today. It is seldom preached and even more uncommonly practiced. But in Job's words: *"Should God then reward you on your terms, when you refuse to repent?"* (Job 34:33).

Paul asked the question: *"Shall we sin because we are not under the law but under grace?"* Then Paul answered his own question: *"By no means!"* (Rom. 6:15). A doctrine of cheap grace rationalizes and minimizes the seriousness of sin and our compromise with culture. It proclaims forgiveness of sins as a general truth, without requiring personal repentance and turning from sin. Cheap grace is the justification of sin, not the justification of the sinner.

Concerning *cheap grace*, Bonheoffer observed, "Cheap grace is the preaching of forgiveness without requiring repentance, baptism without church discipline, communion without confession, absolution without personal confession. Cheap grace is grace without discipleship, grace without the cross, grace without Jesus Christ, living and incarnate."[1]

"Cheap grace" is as popular in the Western church today as repentance is unpopular. It grants "permission" to live however a person wants without feeling guilty or without being accountable to the authority of Christ and God's Word. Cheap grace becomes an "umbrella," a false security covering for sinning and from the consequences of sin.

Attempting to avoid accountability to God by appealing to cheap grace actually separates us from the true grace of mercy and forgiveness, and from the freedom that repentance brings! Without true *grace* there is no true *forgiveness* or cleansing of conscience; therefore, people that rationalize sin rather than repent for it, live under a continual sense of guilt and condemnation.

God, in 2 Chronicles 7:14, instructs believers to humble themselves, pray, and seek God's face, and to turn from their wicked ways. Wicked ways are not just gross transgressions— they are also going our own way. Isaiah describes the essence of sin as:

> All we like sheep have gone astray; We have turned, every one,
> to his own way; And the LORD has laid on Him the iniquity of
> us all (Isa. 53:6 NKJV, emphasis added).

Our own ways are wicked in the sight of God because they are departures from His ways.

The reality of repentance and its importance is everywhere emphasized in the Bible. It may be found in the Old Testament prophets (Jer. 7:3, Ezek. 18:30, Joel 2:12–14, Mal. 3:7), John the Baptist (Matt. 3:2), Jesus Christ (Matt. 4:17; 18:3; Luke 5:32) and New Testament Christians (Acts 2:38; 8:22; 11:18; 2 Pet. 3:9). The New Testament teaches that true repentance will be evident in the fruit of a changed life (Matt. 3:8; Acts 26:20).

The habit of sinning cannot be broken superficially. Sins begin tentatively. When lightning bolts do not fall from the sky after sinning, temptations are indulged more freely. Sin doesn't seem so bad as it did at first. When sin is repeated, the pleasure of sin grows, the conscience is dulled, and a habit develops and tightens its grip. Only true humility and the fire of repentance in response to the Holy Spirit's conviction can break this tight grip of sin in one's life.

God requires the church in the Western world to take steps in turning from our wicked ways before He will answer us from heaven. God in the Scriptures assures us, *"If you repent, I will restore you"* (Jer. 15:19); *"but unless you repent, you will all likewise perish."* (Luke 13:3, ESV).

Three Major Root Sins

There are three major root sins described in the Bible that defile both the individual and the related community where they are condoned. God warns that these sins of will separate us from His presence, protection, and blessing. These sins are especially highlighted in the Old Testament as sins that defile individuals, their community and the land where they live. The three major root sins that the Bible highlights are *idolatry, sexual immorality,* and *shedding of innocent blood.*

The Hebrew prophets all called Israel's leaders and people to repent of these sins. To turn from their wicked ways was insisted on if there was to be national deliverance from impending disaster. The repentance had to be both personal and corporate! This was the burden of the Lord, which all the prophets proclaimed. Mercy and salvation were promised if the people turned from their wicked ways; judgment and disaster were prophesied if they did not turn away from these sins.

Because of the pervasiveness of these issues in our culture and a growing acceptance of them as "normal," even by the church, we must be clear—these issues are contrary to God's Word and ways. We must not accept them as a status quo but recognize they are in the category of rebellion. We have to agree with God on those things that offend Him, not agree with what our culture says about it and therefore consider "normal."

Sin of Idolatry

Foremost among sins that compromise our covenant with God and have dire consequences is the sin of idolatry. Idolatry may be defined as follows: "worshiping, serving, pledging allegiance to, doing acts of obeisance to, paying homage to, forming alliances with, making covenants with, seeking power from, or in any other way exalting any supernatural being other than God."[2]

Thus, it is the first of the Ten Commandments that God gave to Israel (individually and corporately). The New Testament emphasizes that idolatry, if unrepented of, will exclude a person from God's kingdom and presence forever, and will work like poisonous yeast in dough if condoned in the household of faith.

Paul warns us,

> For of this you can be sure: No immoral, impure or greedy person—such a man is an **idolater**—has any inheritance in the kingdom of Christ and of God. Let no one deceive you with empty words, for because of such things God's wrath comes on those who are disobedient (Eph. 5:5–6 [cf. 1 Cor. 6:9–10; 1 Pet. 4:3; Rev. 21:8; 22:15]).

God's timeless moral law in the Ten Commandments explicitly forbids all forms of idolatry (Exod. 20:3–6) for individuals or the community. Idolatry is not confined to worshiping a graven image. The Bible mentions setting up idols in our heart (Ezek. 14:3). The New Testament refers to covetousness as idolatry (Matt. 6:24; Luke 16:13; Col. 3:5; Eph. 5:5). Other things that can be idolatrous are mammon (money, wealth, possessions), the pursuit of pleasure the world's way (often involving parties, alcohol, illicit sex, drugs), giving one's time and affections to television, internet, or other media; idolizing celebrities ("American Idol"), success or status, sports, psychic activity, or occult pursuits. God admonishes His people, *"Repent! Turn from your idols and renounce all your detestable practices!"* (Ezek. 14:6).

Idolatry and Culture

It may seem strange to consider idolatry as an evil associated with our modern world since idols seem only to belong to the ancient world or to pagan cultures. But contemporary Western cultures like the United States, the United Kingdom, and Europe are not only secular and humanistic, but also very idolatrous. God has been replaced with lesser loves.

Let us not flatter ourselves as Christians in thinking that idolatry is beneath us. Idolatry can be anything that we love more than God. A person's heart can be full of idols, even though there are no external objects representing that idolatry. Rich and poor, educated and non-educated, and people of all ethnic backgrounds are guilty of idolatry. Idolatry is a universal sin of humankind and one that brings with it bondage, demons, and curses.

Israel's path to breaking covenant with God almost always involved cultural idolatry, assimilating their neighbor's idolatry. In Jesus' message to the Church of Laodicea, the church looked like the culture in which it lived.

The church (often subtly and unperceived) gradually assimilates the culture in which it exists. The Western culture that began with God has moved to a *culture of humanism* that excludes God from the affairs of life. The church gives token devotion to God on Sunday mornings, but then lives like the idolatrous culture the rest of the time. Then the church still expects God to answer our prayers and bless our lives, family, and church. This was the same pattern of Israel in Old Testament times.

Individual sin is never just personal and hidden. Idolatry always has corporate implications and consequences. Personal sin is often part of a larger cultural pattern of sin that leads to God's corporate judgment.

Haiti used to be a very beautiful and fertile land, and was referred to as "the pearl of the Antilles." Two centuries ago Haiti's leaders made a covenant with Satan. They agreed that if he would deliver Haiti from French rule, they would worship him.

As a result of that idolatrous covenant, voodoo became Haiti's main religion and the land thereafter was cursed. Haiti drastically changed at that point and became the most devastated, poverty-stricken nation in the Western Hemisphere. Such is the curse of idolatry!

Almolonga, a small city of 20,000 tucked in one of the beautiful Guatemalan valleys, became a poverty-stricken community as a result of the idolatrous worship of Maximon and the curse of alcoholism. When transforming revival occurred, Jesus became Lord over the community. As a result, the people, community, and the land is now healed and fertile.

The relationship between idolatry and the consequences that follow is not a myth. The fact that a curse follows idolatry and blessing follows restored covenant with God is a reality that Satan strives to keep hidden.

In the nation of Fiji, along with hundreds of other places in the world, people have begun to recognize the consequences of their idolatry, sin, and ungodly ways. Their communities that were once filled with immorality, crime, poverty, and unfruitful land have now become glorious testimonies of God's redemption of defiled land!

Today the transforming revival sweeping across the nation of Fiji has resulted in amazing changes. In hundreds of Fijian villages, supernatural transformation of the people, society, and land have (and still are) occurring. Repentance and the power of the cross have the potential to break the curse of idolatry at individual, family, and community levels. Yes, even healing the LAND itself! When God's instruction in 2 Chronicles 7:14 is wholeheartedly followed, God promises to *hear from heaven, forgive their sin and heal their land.*

Occult

"Now the Spirit expressly says that in latter times some will depart from the faith, giving heed to deceiving spirits and doctrines of demons," (1 Tim. 4:1 NKJV). Participation in "the occult" is on the rise, which sadly, is indicative of the world's rebellion against God. What's even more serious is that many Christians are caught up in the occult before they realize what they are doing.

It would be impossible to list all of the different forms of occult practices. But here is a short list of some of the most common forms: Horoscopes, New Age, numerology, Ouija boards, out of body experiences, palm reading, psychic readings, reflexology, reincarnation, séances, fortune telling, auras, channeling, charms clairvoyance, communication with crystal balls, crystal healing, any sort of divination, Dungeons & Dragons® and other demonic "games," the Goth and Vampire movement, hypnotism, sorcery spells, summoning demons/spirits, superstition, tarot cards, tea-leaf reading, telepathy, trances, transcendental meditation (TM), interpretation of omens, levitation, magic, mediums, mind control, and astral projection.

God specifically forbids His people from participation in occult activities (Lev. 19:26, 31; Deut. 13:1–3; Deuteronomy

18:9–11; Jeremiah 27:9; 29:8). Participation in the occult is an act of the sinful nature (Gal. 5:19–21) and is a sin (1 Sam. 15:23). It is evil and wickedness (2 Chron. 33:6; Acts 19:17–20; 2 Thes. 2:9–10). It is rebellion against God (Eze. 12:24–25; 21:21–24). It defiles (Lev, 19:31)! The occult is deceiving (Matt. 24:24; Acts 13:8–10; 2 Thessalonians 2:9–10).

False Religions

It is difficult to get accurate estimates of how many witches and pagans are in the United States—200,000 is often a cited figure. A Barnes & Noble marketing executive suggests a Pagan-buying audience of 10 million. Other estimates range as high as 1 million witches and 1 million neo-pagans in the United States.

Witchcraft or *Wiccan's* is officially the fastest growing and legal religion in the United States. United States judges have ruled that witches must be allowed to lead prayers at local government meetings, and that Wiccan convicts must be provided with requested "sacred objects" so they can perform spells while in prison. Witches in the armed services have even formed covens and routinely "worship" on U.S. military bases.

The number of atheists has increased in the past decade from 8% in 1990 to over 14% in 2001. According to Barna Research there are now 35,136,000 atheists in the United States.[3] Other prominent false religions include Islam, which has between 5 to 6 million adherents and the figures are growing. Buddhism which has between 2 to 3 million followers; and Hinduism which has over 1 million adherants.[4]

Mammon

Idolatry in the Western world most certainly involves this god about which Jesus warned. Jesus declared that no one can serve two masters—God and mammon. Mammon is gold, money, wealth, materialism, and affluence. Personified, it's a spirit competing with God Himself. Thus, it is idolatry!

Job says, *"If I have put my trust in gold, . . . I would have been unfaithful to God on high"* (Job 31:24, 28). Job is saying that putting one's trust in money is idolatry. Western nations especially are consumer cultures. As with Sodom and Gomorrah, material abundance creates an obsession for more and more things, while it diminishes the human spirit, over develops soulish appetites, and in the end contributes to a sensual lifestyle of immorality (cf. Ezek 16:49–50; Hos. 1:2; 2:8–9, 12–13; Hag. 1:11).

When will we humble ourselves, repent of being seduced by mammon, turn from our wicked ways, and return to our first love?

Self-Indulgence

Any society that is blessed with abundance gravitates toward indulging the physical appetites. Not surprisingly, a common form of idolatry in the Western world is self-indulgence. Our sinful nature is already bent toward self-centeredness. This condition is intensified by affluence and abundance; and it is worsened by the enticements of demonic spirits. Self-indulgence attracts demons like a picnic draws flies.

Affluence and self-indulgence seem to go together. This was true in Jesus' story about the rich man and Lazarus (Luke 16). It has been true of kings with their wealth and opulence down through history. Now in our Western world, vast populations of people of all classes live an affluent and self-indulgent lifestyle similar to that of kings in ancient history. In many ways abortion is the fruit of a self-indulgent lifestyle.

Western culture has made a god of sinful pleasure. If ancient Greeks or Romans were to see the drunken and sensual weekend parties in the Western world, would they believe that the worship of Bacchus had ceased? If one of them from the past were to see the sexual immorality in society today, would they believe that the worship of Venus had ceased?

The New Testament calls all believers to crucify their sinful and soulish self by being fully identified with Christ at the cross. Furthermore, we are to put aside our old self with its self-centered practices and put on—like a garment—a new redeemed self that *"is being renewed in knowledge in the image of its Creator"* (Col 3:10).

Anything that competes with Jesus for our time and attention can become a substitute for our affections and worship for Him. George Barna reports, "The average congregant spends more time watching television in one day than he spends in all spiritual pursuits combined for an entire week." Where are we spending our time? Or our money? Where are our affections really? Jesus said, "Unless you repent, you will all likewise perish."

Idolatry in the Church

Idolatry was the besetting sin of God's people in the Old Testament. The Old Testament prophets and the book of Revelation explicitly call idolatry spiritual harlotry.

Church traditions can become a source of idolatry. Church tradition gravitates toward becoming a "form" of godliness but without the presence and power of God. Jesus confronted the tradition of Judaism in His day by quoting Isaiah to the Pharisees and scribes:

> *"These people honor me with their lips, but their hearts are far from me. They worship me in vain; their teachings are but rules taught by men"* (Mark 7:6–7).

Then Jesus added,

> *You have a fine way of setting aside the commands of God in order to observe your own traditions! . . . Thus you nullify the word of God by your tradition that you have handed down. And you do many things like that* (Mark 7:9, 13).

The church must intentionally resist the tendency to focus on its religious traditions rather than on Jesus himself. The church must also resist exalting man's teaching and human wisdom or contemporary customs above the revelation and authority of the Bible. Such practices, Jesus said, result in us worshiping Him in vain and nullifying the authority of Scripture by focusing on human tradition.

Denominations by virtue of their unique emphasis on some truth or tradition are susceptible to a sectarian spirit. Focusing on one's denominational tradition rather than focusing worship entirely on Jesus himself is idolatrous. This too we need to repent for and turn from!

The church gets into cultural idolatry when it becomes a subculture rather than a distinctive kingdom culture that is counter to prevailing cultural trends. The church's tendency over time is to assimilate gradually the pattern of sins in its culture almost imperceptibly. In Jesus' message to the Church of Laodicea, the church looked frightfully like the culture in which it lived. He said to the church: *"As many as I love, I rebuke and chasten. Therefore be zealous and repent"* (Rev. 3:19 NKJV).

Ezekiel warns that idolatry of any kind brings reproach to God's name and causes the Lord's glory to depart. In Ezekiel 8–11, God deliberately chose to withdraw His presence and glory from the Temple, the City of Jerusalem, and the nation of Judah because of idolatry. And God held the leaders of God's people responsible. Their idolatry led to the city losing God's presence and the blessings that went with it. Is this not the state of our cities today?

What a sobering reality that God could slowly withdraw His presence from His sanctuary and that it would go unnoticed by those ministering and worshiping there! As a result, God says His ears will no longer hear the cry of the people in the city. Idolatry erects a wall that separates us from God's presence. He will never cross that wall, nor will He ever add His glory in revival to idolatry.

When will the church acknowledge her role and responsibility for our communities' present plight and repent for her own sins? Our personal idolatry contributes to the darkness and devastation in the culture around us. The way out of idolatry is always to repent and turn from our wicked ways! God's people must be ruthless with idolatry before revival from heaven can come!

It is possible to outwardly worship the Lord but also serve our own gods! 2 Kings 17:33 says: *"They [Israel] worshiped the LORD, but they also served their own gods in accordance with the customs of the nations from which they had been brought."* The antidote to idolatry is a surrendered life that loves God wholeheartedly and longs foremost for intimacy with Him.

Sin of Sexual Immorality

God's people are called to be morally and sexually pure (2 Col. 11:2; Titus 2:5; 1 Pet. 3:2). Biblically the word "pure" when referring to sexuality means to be free from all that which is lewd and related to lust. Sexual purity involves refraining from all acts or thoughts (e.g., pornography) that incite sexual desire and passion outside one's marriage covenant or one's virginity before marriage. Purity involves controlling one's own body *"in a way that is holy and honorable"* (1 Thes. 4:4) and is the opposite of *"passionate lust"* (1 Thes. 4:5).

The biblical definition of sexual immorality includes not only forbidden intercourse or consummated acts—such as adultery, sexual intercourse before marriage, homosexuality and lesbianism, and all degrading passions, but also "involves any act of sexual gratification with another person other than one's marriage partner, achieved by uncovering or exploring the nakedness of that person.

The contemporary church teaching that says sexual intimacy among 'committed' unmarried youth and adults is acceptable as long as it stops short of full sexual union is a teaching contrary to God's holiness and the biblical standard of purity. God explicitly prohibits having any kind of 'sexual relations with' (literally, "uncovering the nakedness of") anyone who is not a lawful wife or husband (Lev. 18:6–30; 20:11, 17, 19–21)."[5]

Immorality ignores God's covenant purpose for sexuality and chooses instead to violate God's moral law and another individual. These sins intrude upon the covenant of marriage and always defile the participants. These sins are not only condemned in Scripture, but also place one outside God's kingdom unless repented of and turned away from as "wicked ways" (Rom. 1:24–32; 1 Col. 6:9–10; Gal. 5:19–21).

Immorality and the Culture

Our culture and society pursues and encourages sexual behavior that is forbidden in Scripture and that clearly violates God's love, moral law, and wisdom. Although we have hundreds (sometimes thousands) of churches in most American cities, along with the prevalence of Christian radio and television, America's moral fabric is being shredded. People no longer have a fear of God or a fear of the consequences of sin.

Sexual lifestyles—opposite to those revealed by God in Scripture—are vigorously promoted by Hollywood, TV, news networks, authors, artists, public school teachers, university professors, judges in the courts, internet, and even voices in the church. This new "liberated lifestyle" has produced legal abortion and an epidemic of sexually transmitted diseases, moral chaos, and is leading the United States and other West-ern nations down the road of moral suicide.

"Sex" is now the number 1 topic searched on the Internet. Child pornography generates $3 billion annually and The Na-tional Coalition for the Protection of Children and Families states that, "approximately 40 million people in the United States are sexually involved with the Internet."[6] These statis-tics reveal that there is both a national and global obsession with sex and perversion apart from the context of marriage covenant and thus apart from God.

Sexual immorality is now viewed as normal behavior in the Western world. Caution about sexual promiscuity gener-ally revolves around the issue of sexually transmitted diseases or unwanted pregnancy. Modern education and our culture generally are not really concerned about devastating emo-tional entanglements or personal integrity or dishonoring God—just venereal disease.[7] God's moral wisdom and law are viewed as archaic and now unacceptable.

What are the consequences of moral relativity and remov-ing God from society's way of life? "In America, as in other nations, it has led to the destruction of the family unit, the silencing of the voice of God's people, the development of a widespread culture of sexual immorality, hedonism, material-ism, abortion, and the rejection of Christ in the public place—resulting in "an epidemic of sexual perversion, sexual abuse of children, same sex marriage, and other morally reprehen-sible behavior.

"Unless a massive spiritual shift occurs…our children will live under an antichrist system and godless enculturation that will bring about the demise of America as we know it. . . . Now is the time for key men and women, even an entire gen-eration, to risk everything to become the hinge of history, the pivotal point that determines which way the door will swing in America and in the nations of the earth."[8]

Immorality in the Church

The church in recent years has been riddled with incidents of immorality among leaders. Hardly a day goes by that we don't hear a charge of sexual abuse, corruption, or moral failure among members of the clergy. The Lord is exposing the church's sin, just as the prophet Hosea warned: *"I will uncover her lewdness in the sight of her lovers"* (Hos. 2:10 ESV).

Widespread immorality in the church has weakened her authority and credibility to speak about issues like morality, honesty, and family. Why should the world believe our message when churches ordain practicing homosexuals and lesbians, and permit gay bishops to preside over church regions?

The prevalent visiting of online pornography by people who regard themselves as born again Christians is astonishing. A Promise Keepers survey found that over seventy-five percent of the Christian men interviewed have struggled with Internet pornography. Sixty-three percent of men attending "Men, Romance & Integrity Seminars" admit to struggling with pornography during a recent year. Two-thirds are in church leadership.[9]

God exhorts his people, *"get rid of all moral filth and the evil **that is so prevalen**t and humbly accept the word planted in you, which can save you"* (Jas. 1:21, emphasis added).

Peter adds:

> For you have spent enough time in the past doing what pagans choose to do--living in debauchery, lust, drunkenness, orgies, carousing and detestable idolatry. They think it strange that you do not plunge with them into the same flood of dissipation, and they heap abuse on you. But they will have to give account to him who is ready to judge the living and the dead (1 Pet. 4:3–5).

Current history is reminding us of another fact. When God's people take seriously God's instruction in 2 Chronicles 7:14 by humbling themselves, praying and seeking God's face, repenting and turning from their wicked ways, God still hears from heaven, still forgives the sin of a repentant community, and still is willing to heal our land. We have current convincing proof from hundreds of transformed communities that God still responds to his people who humble themselves, pray, and repent.

Sin of Shedding of Innocent Blood

After Cain murdered his righteous brother Abel, God said to Cain, *"What have you done? Listen! Your brother's blood cries out to me from the ground. Now you are under a curse and driven from the ground, which opened its mouth to receive your brother's blood from your hand"* (Gen. 4:10–11).

God will avenge the blood of the innocent and will not forget. The Psalmist declares, *"For he who avenges blood remembers; he does not ignore the cry of the afflicted"* (Psa. 9:12). Shedding of innocent blood registers on the conscience as a staggering burden (1 Sam. 25:30–34).

The shedding of innocent blood is a huge issue with God. Bloodshed and violence have always drawn God's wrath and judgment as in the days of Noah.

> *"Now the earth was corrupt in God's sight and was full of violence. . . . So God said to Noah, 'I am going to put an end to all people, for the earth is filled with violence because of them. I am surely going to destroy both them and the earth'"* (Gen. 6:11, 13).

God abhors violence and shedding of innocent blood under both the old covenant and new covenant. It was not just an issue for Cain, Noah's generation, or Israel as a nation under the law; it is also an issue for all people and nations under the governance of the Creator and Judge of all the earth.

Psalm 106 discusses the consequences of rebellion and the issue of defilement that comes from idolatry, sexual immorality, and the shedding of innocent blood. As Israel mingled with the nations and conformed to their culture, idolatry began to ensnare them and their families.

> *They sacrificed their sons and their daughters to demons. They shed innocent blood, the blood of their sons and daughters, . . . and the **land was desecrated** by their blood. They **defiled themselves** by what they did"* (Psa. 106:37–39a, emphasis added).

Defilement, like sin, begins at an individual level and defiles the person. But sin does not stop with the individual; it contributes to corporate sin and community defilement. The very earth groans as a result of our compounding iniquity. Psalm 106:43 says, *"they were bent on rebellion and they wasted away in their sin."* Even as this happens for individuals, it happens for families, communities, and even the land.

God makes it clear in His Word that He will *"hide His eyes"* from us when we pray if our *"hands are full of blood"* (Isa. 1:15). Violence and bloodshed are a primary reason for God's presence remaining at a distance from His people. The shedding of innocent blood defiles people and land; and it cries out for justice as did Abel's blood. No human institutions or government can deliver us from the impact of such serious sin on society.

Nahum 3:1 says, *"Woe to the city of blood."* Blood here represents innocent bloodshed, murder, and violence resulting in death. Bloodshed pollutes and defiles, and must be atoned for before God's presence can return. Judgment and devastation are the inevitable consequences of a land being full of bloodshed, and of a city being full of violence and injustice. *"Prepare chains, because the land is full of bloodshed and the city is full of violence* (Ezek. 7:23).

God looks for righteousness and justice in His people. When He sees bloodshed and hears cries of distress instead, He waits for righteous intercessors and mediators to act before

He can respond in restoration and transformation.

In biblical times, some in Israel and Judah were offering their babies as sacrifices to the god Molech. In South and Central America, the Inca, Aztec, and Mayan people sacrificed their babies to the their gods. In contemporary history, people all over the world are now sacrificing their babies to the same demonic spirits as a consequence of their lust for pleasure, convenience, and a self-indulgent lifestyle.

The killing of unborn babies is the ultimate shedding of innocent blood. When we think of all the war casualties in all the American wars combined, awful as that is, it does not begin to compare to the massive number of babies murdered annually around the world. The total number of legally sanctioned abortions of infants in the United States alone since 1973 is now at 50,000,000. The church's participation in this is not small. One in six women who have had abortions are reportedly "evangelical Christians."[10]

Idolatry eventually becomes a systemic issue for society and culture. Sin—whether idolatry, sexual immorality, or innocent bloodshed as in abortion—is neither simply an individual choice nor its consequences confined to the person who transgresses. When we sin, we contribute to the spiritual darkness of our community, its defilement, and moral decline. Individual sin sows into the corporate problem and empowers the demonic principality over our community, city, and geographical region.

Corporate Repentance

Corporate sin brings corporate consequences and corporate judgment. Corporate repentance brings corporate blessing and God's favor in transforming revival. We desperately need leaders who will lead the way in a revival of corporate repentance in our communities.

The revival needs to be as seriously focused as the one at Nineveh when Jonah preached repentance to it. The Nineveh revival may be the single most remarkable revival of repentance in history. One reason it was so remarkable is that it started with the top ruler humbling himself and leading the city in repentance (Jon. 4:7–10).

The pagan king of Nineveh demonstrated the kind of humility and repentance that must come to our churches, if there is to be any hope of community-wide revival from heaven. Nineveh's king was resolutely humble, urgent in seeking God's forgiveness, and decisive in turning from his and the city's wicked ways in hope that God's fierce wrath and destruction might be averted and the city saved.

How can church and civic leaders in our communities do any less than Nineveh's king and still hope that our children, youth, spouses, churches, and communities will be spared destruction? How can the church persist with the status quo and with life as usual, and reasonably expect that we will somehow be exempt from the consequences of our present ways?

Only the cleansing fire of repentance and the blood of Jesus can deal with the problems that the church and cities are now facing. Twice Jesus warned, *"Unless you repent, you will all likewise perish"* (Luke 13:3 ESV). These words were not primarily spoken to Gentile sinners or pagans, but to the Jews, God's covenant people, who were religious but not righteous.

Presently idolatry, immorality, bloodshed, and violence *are causing a wasting and shriveling of life* (cf. Hos. 4:1–3) at all levels—the individual and family levels, the church level, societal level and the national level. Leaders and cities bring on themselves devastation and finally destruction when there is no corporate repentance for these sins. God warns that He will not spare His judgment unless His people turn from their wicked ways, stand in the breach, and intercede for God's merciful intervention.

Corporate Repentance in Papau New Guinea

The Makirupu Village only has a population of about 600 but had a terrible reputation of disputes between churches and families. During the transformation process, the ministry team learned that three previous pastors in the village had committed adultery and fornication in the past 30 years. The last incident involved a young girl and the sin occurred behind the pulpit in the church building. A court case was brought by the elders but the young girl insisted she was innocent. The whole village became embroiled in the case and almost all of the young people left the church as a result. The life and attendance of the church suffered. The sin was like a dark shadow hovering over the church, the people and the village.

During the process of repentance the current pastor stood in the gap and repented on behalf of the three former pastors for the adultery and fornication. Then others stepped forward and they each identified and repented for immorality and their involvement in and the presence of the Lord began to rest heavily on the church.

Finally, shaking and trembling under the fear of the Lord and great conviction, the young girl who had been accused of engaging in the immorality with the pastor came forward and began to confess and repent and asked forgiveness from the Lord and the whole village.

The next day the spiritual atmosphere was changed and all the young people came back to church and it was filled to capacity! The fear of the Lord entered the hearts of the people. Church leaders began to reconcile for their divisions. News spread through the village and to nearby villages and many more hungry people gathered to hear the word of the Lord and seek healing for their own families and villages. Signs and wonders began to occur something the people had never witnessed before and the revival began.

The final day the entire village was dedicated to the Lord and anointed by the leaders as God continued to cleanse and heal their land. Many items of idolatry were burned in a large bonfire, more families were reconciled, husbands and wives were reconciled as God cleaned up the lives of the people! Many miracles began to occur as people repented for their sin and were reconciled to God and each other![11]

Taking Responsibility

Daniel was a humble and wise leader who led the way among the Jewish exiles in humility, intercession, and repentance. As a leader, Daniel did not point the finger of accusation at the Jewish people; rather he took responsibility by identifying with his people's sin:

> *We have sinned and committed iniquity, we have done wickedly and rebelled, even by departing from Your precepts and Your judgments. Neither have we heeded Your servants the prophets, who spoke in Your name to our kings and our princes, to our fathers and all the people of the land. O Lord, righteousness belongs to You, but to us shame of face, as it is this day* (Dan. 9:5-7 NKJV).

As Daniel was humbling himself, seeking God's face, repenting of sin, and appealing for God to relent His judgment on the City of Jerusalem, the angel Gabriel was sent by God to give Daniel insight and understanding. *"As soon as you began to pray, an answer was given . . . for you are highly esteemed"* (Dan. 9:23, emphasis added).

God highly esteems leaders who will humble themselves and take responsibility for the mess that they and their cities are in! Other leaders in Scripture who did this were David, Isaiah, Hezekiah, Ezra, Nehemiah. When they faced distressful situations, they humbled themselves and led the way in repentance.

Godly leaders do not project blame on others for their present spiritual crisis. Rather, they take responsibility for their own sin and the sins of their forefathers in order to find God's solution for the situation they are in.

Pastors who are willing to repent of their own sins and to lead their family members into repentance, will then have authority and credibility to lead their congregation into repentance and into revival. Desperation and humility that results in seeking God's face and in true repentance by leaders will become contagious when modeled before their people. Humility and leading by example are powerful principles in God's kingdom.

Scripture is clear—God resolutely opposes those who are proud, stubborn, and have an unrepentant heart, but He always gives much grace to leaders and people who humble themselves and repent. Leaders who fail (for whatever reason) to lead the way in humility and repentance with their spouse and family, cannot expect repentance to be a reality in their congregation. The church desperately needs a revival of repentance and this revival must start with leaders.[12]

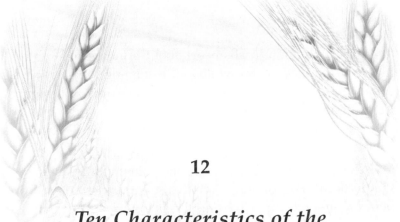

12

Ten Characteristics of the Coming Great Revival

*And it shall come to pass in the last days, says God, that I will pour out
of My Spirit on ["all flesh" NKJV] ["all people" NIV]*

Acts 2:17, (emphasis added)

God's purposeful progression in revival eras will climax
in what Robert Coleman calls "The Coming World Revival."[1] The accumulative biblical and historical evidence for
a great global revival near the end of the age is strong. Recognizing the complexity of looking into the future in biblical
prophecies on the one hand and of assessing the contemporary indicators on the other hand, still leads us to convincing
evidence of a future great revival "that will make anything
seen thus far pale by comparison."[2]

We may be in the beginning of the beginning of the end-time revival in some locations, but the vastness of this revival
is still ahead of us! We presently have the privilege of partnering with God the Father in the final preparation of the ages for
the coming again of the Lord Jesus and the great revival that
precedes His coming.

It is an inadequate understanding of biblical revelation to
believe that history ends in the global supremacy of evil until
Jesus returns. God intends to fulfill every promise in His Word

and every intention in His heart about bringing redemptive history to fullness, even while evil is coming to its fullness. The coming great revival will play a major role in bringing to fulfillment the promises in Scripture about a fully mature church (Eph. 4:13) and a fully global harvest of the nations (Rev. 7:9).

What is the biblical, historical, and contemporary evidence that indicates the coming of another great worldwide revival before Christ returns? Here are 10 reasons for and characteristics of the coming final great revival.

1. Great Global Groundswell of Prayer

Without great prayer, there can be no great revival! Based on the precedent of revival history, we would expect a great revival on a global scale to be preceded by a massive swell of extraordinary prayer for revival on a global scale. This is exactly what is happening in the twenty-first century; widespread intercession for revival is increasing rapidly.

In 1997, Bill Bright, founder of Campus Crusade for Christ, called belivers in the United States to a 40-day fast for revival in our nation. He believed that if we would fast and pray, God would release a vast revival. God did not release that revival immediately, but He did release a revival of prayer on a much larger scale, both in scope and in intensity, as a result of the many who prayed and fasted for those 40 days in 1997.

A global tidal wave of prayer for revival that is unprecedented in church history is rising. Forty years ago no one was talking about citywide, nationwide and worldwide corporate 40-day fasts for revival. It was commonly thought that 21-day and 40-day fasts were only done in Bible times. Today lengthy fasts like these are occurring frequently and participated in widely, especially by the younger generation who see and understand that a massive revival is coming. Natural hunger pains from these fasts are being translated by the Spirit into gut wrenching spiritual hunger for Jesus and His kingdom. God's kingdom is at the door and ready to break out in unprecedented holiness and power.

Widespread Prayer for Revival

God is inspiring unprecedented prayer for an unprecedented revival in a time of unprecedented trouble in the earth. Passionate groups of fiery intercessors are gathering in cities and nations in Africa, Asia, Europe, Russia, the Middle East, South–Central–North America, Australia, and New Zealand—actually on all continents and on many islands around the world. What began as localized, regional, and national intercessory bonfires are now great conflagrations globally.

One prominent indicator of this global trend is the Global Day of Prayer which provides intercession for spiritual awaken ing and has organized visible expressions of prayer worldwide each Spring since 2002. Different prayer streams across the globe blend and flow together in agreement for the manifest presence of God and His glory to come to every community and nation on the earth.

This amazing expression of prayer is still expanding worldwide. In 2006, millions of Christians from 199 nations united in prayer; in 2008 even more Christians from 214 nations participated; in 2010 multiplied millions gathered to pray and worship in over 200 nations. That is global prayer!

Another groundswell of prayer began in England in 1999 with a single night-and-day prayer room and subsequently has grown into an international, interdenominational, youth movement committed to prayer, mission, and justice. Envisioned by Pete Greig who is the International Director of **24-7 Prayer,** this movement has and is impacting youth, college campuses, and churches in Europe, United States, and beyond.

Since the year 2000, **The Call**, led by Lou Engle has been a national and international call to prayer—especially for youth and young adults. The Call has gathered in stadiums in a dozen nations and many major cities (e.g., Washington D.C. 400,000 on the Mall; 100,000 New York City; 70,000 Nashville; etc.) to worship and intercede for national revival and global spiritual awakening. The cry of intercession is that God will break societal strongholds of evil like immorality, abortion, gay marriage and stem the tide of humanism.

Large **solemn assemblies** of people praying and fasting for revival and spiritual awakening are occurring periodically in nations around the world. In Nigeria on Fridays every month, one million people gather for united prayer for revival and the invasion of God's kingdom on earth as it is in heaven. The prayers of the saints like incense literally arise night and day from all over the earth to heaven's throne room in a measure unprecedented in history. The stage is being set for the greatest revival from heaven ever!

Houses of Prayer Worldwide

In 1999, the **International House of Prayer in Kansas City** (IHOP-KC) officially opened its doors as a house of continual prayer and worship 24 hours a day. From dawn to dusk, through the night watches, and every holiday, prayer and worship continues 24 hours a day, 7 days a week, 365 days a year. This prayer is not a fad but a lifestyle!

Mike Bickle, founder and director of IHOP-KC, was given by the Lord in 1982 "four heart standards" to which God said he was to be committed throughout his ministry. The acronym (IHOP) represents for Bickle these four heart standards God gave him: Intercession, Holiness, Offerings for the poor, and Prophetic revelation. The acronym now serves a double purpose as the International House Of Prayer for a large and growing prayer/worship community.

This unique prayer-sanctuary is saturated with the presence of God as night and day worship and prayer mingle together as incense that arises to the throne of God. The majority of the intercessors in the prayer room are young adults who are crying out for revival in the church and for spiritual awakening in cities and nations.

Recently, the International House of Prayer and *God TV* formed a partnership to broadcast the 24/7 prayer room live every day into the living rooms of homes in 160 nations, spreading spiritual hunger and intercession. This live webcast enables thousands of intercessors—in places like Egypt, Israel, Iraq, the Middle East, and nations the world over—to connect to the prayer furnace and fan the flames of intercession for revival in every nations! Even closed nations are connecting so that there is now no such thing as a "closed nation" any longer.

At the beginning and near the end of Jesus' earthly ministry, He forcefully cleansed the Jerusalem Temple and declared, *"My house will be called a house of prayer"* (Matt. 21:12–13; John 2:12–25; cf., Isa. 56:7). Immediately after Jesus cleansed the Temple, the Scripture states "the blind and the lame came to Him at the temple and He healed them" (Matt. 21:14).

When the church again becomes a house of prayer, we will again see Jesus healing all manner of disease and infirmity there. Extraordinary prayer always precedes extraordinary visitations of God among His people. When God's house is no longer a house of prayer, God's presence withdraws to a distance and the supernatural manifestations of His presence ceases.

God is reemphasizing in this century the priority of prayer and literal "Houses of Prayer" are springing-up in cities and nations worldwide. In Jerusalem alone, a city of approximately 850,000 population, there are eight Christian "houses of prayer," some of which are 24/7.

In cities where houses of prayer/worship are planted and take root, light, righteousness, and protection will increase. In cities where no prayer and worship is ascending day and night to God's throne, darkness, and evil will increase and prevail.

The days are coming when it will be frightfully dangerous to live in cities where there is no great corporate prayer effort. The cost of a prayerless and lukewarm church will be great darkness in cities as it presently is; but in the end-time the cost will be disastrous and include certain judgments. It will be like Lot and his family living in Sodom where darkness was dense and judgment was at the door.

Righteousness and light will get more intense for the Bride waiting in intimacy and prayer. At the same time evil and darkness will get more intense in prayerless and humanistic environments. The time for great prayer, resolve, and commitment by the global body of Christ is now. The coming great revival will be fueled by extraordinary prayer and worship!

2. *Great Army of Forerunner Messengers*

As the culmination of redemptive history gets nearer, the activity and ministry of the Holy Spirit on the earth is intensifying. Just as God raised up John the Baptist as a forerunner messenger to prepare the way for Jesus' first coming, so God will raise up a generation of young forerunners whose primary purpose in life is to prepare the way for Jesus' second coming. Just as a great revival occurred with the forerunner message of John the Baptist before Jesus' first coming, so a great revival will occur with the forerunner message before Jesus' second coming.

We may actively partner with God as He brings history to a grand salvific conclusion; or we can sit on the sidelines and be consumed with ourselves! An editorial in *Christianity Today* magazine observes that many young Western evangelicals [like their elders] have succumbed to a lifestyle of comfort and cultural acceptance, rather than a lifestyle of radical disciple-ship that conforms only to Jesus Christ. The relentless voice of media and public education about the legitimacy of alterna-tive sexual lifestyles has largely succeeded in compromising church youth. "Cultural acceptance, today, is their paramount desire."[3]

These younger evangelicals tend to imitate cultural trends of pleasure and entertainment in order to win temporal ac-ceptance for [themselves and] the church, but their converts to Jesus and His kingdom are few. Not only few converts, but also anemic ones! Since they themselves fail to embrace the costly kingdom lifestyle that Jesus sets forth in the Sermon on the Mount, their converts likewise fail to do so.

But a new breed of youthful forerunner messengers is now arising who are willing to pay the cost of discipleship (Sermon on the Mount lifestyle) in order to fully engage with God's end-time agenda! This new generation of committed Jesus-disciples that God is raising up *are diligent* in praying daily (connecting with God while changing their world), in embracing the spiritual discipline of weekly fasting (so as to position themselves to freely receive more from God), and in dedicating themselves to godly justice and righteous deeds that exalt Jesus.

This new breed is choosing a fasted-lifestyle of simplic-ity—with prayer, worship, and fasting being the core focus of everything they do for Him. These younger forerunner mes-sengers are finding joy in giving extravagantly to the poor, are committing to live holy lives that are fascinated with loving God with all their being, are leading diligently by taking the initiative to minister to others, and are willing to boldly speak the truth as faithful witnesses of Jesus Christ.[4]

Forerunner messengers are rising in China, South Korea, and other parts of Asia and boldly witnessing to Muslims along the "Silk Road" from China to Istanbul. Many of these messengers have as their goal the bringing of the gospel back full circle to Israel, Jerusalem, and the Middle East. Forerunners carry the conviction that Jesus is returning and they are messengers who will help prepare the way for His second coming, as John the Baptist did for Jesus' first coming.

A great revival will occur before Jesus' second coming, just as it did with John the Baptist before Jesus' first coming. What an awesome hour of history to be intimate friends of the Bridegroom during this late hour and to be forerunners for Him. Forerunner messengers will proclaim Jesus' second coming, will listen to and hear what the Spirit is saying, "will imitate the simple, fasted lifestyle of John the Baptist and the New Testament apostles who rejected the professional robes of religion for a lifestyle of obedience to Jesus and walking in the power of the Spirit."[5]

We should not think it strange that God would send forerunner messengers before Jesus' second coming, just as He did before Jesus' first coming. These messengers will carry revival fire and be a clear prophetic voice and testimony to the end-time generation.

3. Great Global Outpouring

The Promise

God extends His kingdom to the whole world. Jesus said that His church in the end-time would proclaim the gospel of the kingdom (i.e., Jesus' kingdom message accompanied by healing and deliverance) *in the whole world to **all nations*** and then the end will come (Matt. 24:14). Likewise, Joel's prophecy emphatically promises a global outpouring of the Holy Spirit with great salvation at the very end of history. God speaking through Joel says:

> *And afterward, I will pour out my Spirit on **all people**. Your sons and daughters will prophesy, your old men will dream*

> *dreams, your young men will see visions. Even on my servants,*
> *both men and women, I will pour out my Spirit in those days.*
> *I will show wonders in the heavens and on the earth, blood and*
> *fire and billows of smoke. The sun will be turned to darkness and*
> *the moon to blood before the coming of the great and dreadful*
> *day of the LORD. **And everyone who calls on the name of***
> ***the LORD will be saved*** (Joel 2:28–32a, emphasis added).

The promise includes "all nations" and "all people," and the salvation response of "everyone who calls" on Jesus is potentially vast.

As in Noah's Day

Jesus says the worldwide situation in the end-time will be "as in the days of Noah" (Matt. 24:36–39a; cf., Luke 17:26–27). In Noah's day (generation), Noah and his extended family were prepared, "saved," and spared destruction at the time of the great Genesis flood judgment. Because Jesus used the "days of Noah" specifically to illustrate that judgment is coming for those unprepared, most interpreters focus only on this negative implication of "Noah's day" for those living at the end-time. But the implications of "as in the days of Noah" are broader.

The worldwide destructive flood in the time of Noah is described in Genesis this way:

> *On that day all the springs of the great deep burst forth* [i.e.,
> "all the underground waters erupted from the earth"—
> NLT], *and the floodgates of the heavens were opened. And rain*
> *fell on the earth forty days and forty nights* (Gen. 7:11–12).

The Bible emphasizes that in Noah's day *the physical flood covered the entire earth,* not simply one region of the earth (Gen. 7:4; 2 Pet. 2:5; 3:6). Only Noah's family survived in the whole earth. As a global "physical flood" happened in the natural realm in ancient times, so *a global flood of the Spirit* is prophesied for the end-time (Joel 2:28). This much is clear—the physical flood of Noah's day was worldwide; the spiritual flood at the end-time will likewise be worldwide!

Genesis 7:11 provides a prophetic clue to the enormous magnitude of the end-time outpouring of the Holy Spirit. The Bible describes the Genesis flood as being precipitated by eruptions of great reservoirs of water locked beneath the earth's surface, combined with a universal deluge of physical rain from above—all of which led to a flood of unprecedented global destruction.

The Bible prophesies that in the end-time supernatural streams of life-giving water will erupt and flow from within Spirit-filled believers like "rivers" (John 7:38–39; 14:12–14), combined with a universal deluge of the Holy Spirit like spiritual rain from heaven. This twofold release of the Holy Spirit's presence and power will result in an unprecedented flood of salvation on the earth.

Supporting Evidence

The biblical support for this great end-time flood of the Spirit is often overlooked. It has support, however, in both the Old and New Testaments. Among the many statements in the Psalms and Old Testament prophets, the following are exemplary.

In **Isaiah 32**, the prophet exhorts his listeners:

> Beat your breasts for the pleasant fields, for the fruitful vines . . . till the Spirit is poured [like rain] upon us from on high, and the desert becomes a fertile field, and the fertile field seems like a forest (Isa. 32:12, 15).

In prophetic language, the life-giving flood of the Spirit like rain transforms the landscape from a desert to a luscious, fertile land and forest.

The past 100 years, regional outpourings of the Spirit have occurred in revival history, resulting in widespread spiritual awakening. But in Isaiah 32, the prophet instructs us to pray for an outpouring that is no longer partial but full, that transforms the spiritual landscape like a physical desert would be transformed into a green forest.

This same imagery is used by the prophet in **Isaiah 35**. There Isaiah prophesies a fullness of time when:

> *The desert and the parched land will be glad; the wilderness will rejoice and blossom. Like the crocus, it will burst into bloom (Isa. 35:1–2a).* [God's people] *will see the glory of the LORD, the splendor of our God.* [Because] *[w]ater will gush forth in the wilderness and streams in the desert. The burning sand will become a pool, the thirsty ground bubbling springs* (Isa. 35:2b, 6–7, emphasis added).

When the Spirit comes globally like rain, a vast spiritual outpouring occurs with great healing and creative miracles as in the ministry of Jesus and the early church. Thus, Isaiah adds, *"Then will the eyes of the blind be opened and the ears of the deaf unstopped. Then will the lame leap like a deer, and the mute tongue shout for joy"* (Isa. 35:5–6).

The end-time fulfillment of the great Spirit-flood in Isaiah 35 fits well with the Joel 2 description of a worldwide flood of the Spirit in the end-time.

> *"And afterward, I will pour out my Spirit on all people . . . I will show wonders in the heavens and on the earth, . . . And everyone who calls on the name of the LORD will be saved . . ."* (Joel 2:28, 30, 32).

The Joel passage indicates that the global outpouring of the Spirit will impact representatives of all classes of people around the world. Joel mentions "all people," "sons and daughters," "old men and young men," "servants and handmaids" which encompass the whole range of people and classes.

Eschatological Signs

Among the strongest and most indisputable biblical evidence of a great end-time revival is Joel's prophecy about a global outpouring of the Holy Spirit. The eschatological signs that will be occurring in the heavens and on the earth are mentioned in the *context of Jesus' return.*

Peter in **Acts 2:16–17** quoted the Joel 2 promise as beginning to be fulfilled with the outpouring of the Holy Spirit at Pentecost. But Pentecost was the beginning, not the end; it was a partial fulfillment of Joel 2. The fullness will include people literally all over the world at a time when eschatological wonders are occurring in the heavens and powerful signs are occurring on the earth immediately preceding Jesus' return (Joel 2:30-31; Matt. 24:29; Mark 13:24–26; Luke 21:25–27; Rev. 6:12–13).

Neither the eschatological nor global dimensions of Joel's prophecy were fulfilled at Pentecost. The rain or outpouring of the Spirit that happened at the first Pentecost was the firstfruits. It also foreshadowed the global rain or outpouring of the Spirit when the eschatological wonders in the heaven and signs on the earth will be occurring.

Many have associated the twentieth century outpouring of the Holy Spirit worldwide with the fullness of what Joel 2 promised. But in the twentieth century outpouring that has been truly worldwide, there still were no *"wonders in the heavens and on the earth, blood and fire and billows of smoke. The sun . . .* [did not turn] *to darkness and the moon to blood"* as Joel 2:30–31 and Acts 2:17–20 predict.

Jesus Himself places these Joel 2 cosmic signs in the context of the days *immediately after the tribulation* (NASB; NKJV) at which time *the sun will be darkened, and the moon will not give its light; the stars will fall from the sky, and the heavenly bodies will be shaken* (Matt. 24:29; cf., Rev. 6:12–13). At the end of the age,

God will summon the forces of nature (heavenly and earthly) to bear witness to what is happening on the earth in the global outpouring and the end-time revival, thereby signaling the time for Jesus' return.

This final revival from heaven will surpass all previous historic revivals and in fact be the accumulative sum of them all. In the midst of dense darkness and fervent hatred of Jesus' true followers, the coming great revival will explode globally. The revival will crescendo as a Spirit-flood when God's people are crying out globally for more rain of the Spirit at the time of the latter rain as in Zechariah 10:1—*Ask the LORD for rain in the time of the latter rain. The LORD will make flashing clouds; He will give them . . . rain* (NKJV).

4. Great Trouble on the Earth

God's love and redemption will extend to the whole world right up to the end. The eschatological context in Joel 2, Matthew 24, and Revelation 6–17 is the setting for both the global outpouring of the Spirit in fullest measure, as well as the occurrence of great trouble on the earth in unprecedented measure. Great revival and massive harvest will occur at a time when cities are in great crises and nations in unprecedented chaos. The Bible gives us no reason to believe that the coming great revival will avert God's judgments or global chaos.

During this time, food shortages, contagious plagues and natural disasters of staggering proportions will be happening on the earth and causing men's hearts to fail from fear. During this time global government will seek to manage and control the earth under the leadership of a global leader. Hate will fill the hearts of multitudes. Moral law will so break down that no one will feel safe. Unprecedented pressure to conform to governmental decrees (that are in conflict to loyalty to Jesus) will cause political correctness to prevail as the only acceptable behavior. All the religions of the world will come together under one banner.

The end-time will be the worst time to live if you don't know Jesus; but it will be the greatest time to live for those who do know Him. It will be the church's noblest hour in all-church history. The cost of discipleship will be high and the number of martyrs many. Yet in the midst of very grim times, the Bible indicates that *everyone who calls on the name of the LORD will be saved* (Joel 2:32). And many in trouble will call out to God and be saved as revival sweeps across the earth.

Fearful conditions and dreadful calamities, along with awesome displays of God's power and salvation, will actually create an environment for earnest heart-searching. When God's judgments are in the earth, the inhabitants of the world will learn righteousness (Isaiah 26:9). Not everyone will turn to God, but perhaps a tithe of the world's population will. The vast majority will remain unrepentant and become even more brazen in their sin. But the world will be made to confront as never before the reality of the God-man, Christ Jesus, and His Kingdom.[6]

5. Great Miracles, Signs and Wonders

The ministry of the early church in the beginning was exactly the same as the ministry of Jesus. The ministry of the church in the coming great revival will again look like Jesus' ministry. There was a direct correlation between the early church's signs, wonders, miracles and their effective proclamation of the gospel which is clearly indicated in Acts. In the end-time, the proclamation of Jesus worldwide will again be accompanied with powerful signs, wonders and great salvation as in the New Testament.

Signs and wonders will increase in quantity and magnitude as Jesus predicted in John 14:12–14, more so during the end-time conflict between God and Satan than at any other time of history. As manifestation of human depravity increases globally, so manifestation of God's redemptive light will cover the earth.

- *Everyone was filled with awe, and* **many** *wonders and miraculous signs were done by the apostles. . . . And the Lord added to their number daily those who were being saved* (Acts 2:43, 47b, emphasis added).

- *Stephen [not an apostle], a man full of God's grace and power, [also] did* **great** *wonders and miraculous signs among the people* (Acts 6:8, emphasis added).

- *Phillip [one of the 7 in Acts 6:5, also not an apostle] went down to the city of Samaria and preached Christ to them. And the multitudes with one accord heeded the things spoken by Philip,* **hearing and seeing the miracles** *which he did. For unclean spirits, crying with a loud voice, came out of many who were possessed; and many who were paralyzed and lame were healed. And there was* **great joy in that city** (Acts 8:4–8 NKJV, emphasis added).

- *As Peter traveled throughout Judea encouraging believers, he came to a town named Lydda. There he found a certain man named Aeneas, who had been bedridden eight years and was paralyzed. And Peter said to him, "Aeneas, Jesus the Christ heals you. Arise and make your bed." Then he arose immediately. So* **all who dwelt at Lydda and Sharon** *saw him and turned to the Lord* (Acts 9:33–35 NKJV, emphasis added).

This same direct correlation between healing, signs, miracles and the effective preaching of Jesus—with multitudes believing on Him for salvation—will characterize the church in the coming great revival. Great signs and wonders by God through His people during a time of great trouble will increase exponentially the response of unbelievers to the gospel.

The Psalmist understood the importance of the manifestation of God's power. He had a non-Western worldview and a non-cessationist theology about the power of God:

> *Summon your power, O God; show us your strength, O God,*
> *as you have done before. . . . Proclaim the power of God, . . .You*
> *are awesome, O God, in your sanctuary; the God of Israel gives*
> *power and strength to his people* (Psa. 68:28, 34a, 35, empha-
> sis added).

> *I will come a nd proclaim your mighty acts, O Sovereign LORD.*
> *. . . To this day I declare your marvelous deeds. Even when I am*
> *old and gray, do not forsake me, O God, till I declare your power*
> *to the next generation, your might to all who are to come* (Psa.
> 71:16–18, emphasis added).

When God did great signs and wonders through Daniel and his three friends in Babylon, King Nebuchadnezzar
(aware of these things) in a time of great trouble (7 years of
insanity) encountered their God and penned these words:

> *To the peoples, nations and men of every language, who live in*
> *all the world . . . It is my pleasure to tell you about the miracu-*
> *lous signs and wonders that the Most High God has performed*
> *for me.* **How great are his signs, how mighty his wonders!**
> *His kingdom is an eternal kingdom; his dominion endures from*
> *generation to generation* (Dan. 4:1–3, emphasis added).

Great signs and wonders in the midst of great trouble and
adversity will cause many to take notice of God who would
not do so otherwise. The coming great revival will be punc-
tuated with great signs and mighty wonders in the midst of
great darkness as spoken of in Isaiah 60. Isaiah prophesies:

> *See, darkness covers the earth and thick darkness is over the peo-*
> *ples, but the LORD rises upon you and his glory appears over*
> *you. Nations will come to your light, and kings to the bright-*
> *ness of your dawn* (60:2-3).

The initial fulfillment of Isaiah 60 that occurred at Jesus'
first coming (Matt. 4:12–17) will be surpassed in the end-time
both in terms of the thickness of darkness and of the widespread manifestations of God's glory made plain through miraculous signs and wonders.

In the coming great revival, *"knowledge of the* [manifest] *glory of God"* will be widespread; in fact it *"will cover the earth"* (Hab. 2:14) at a time of great "woe" judgments (Hab. 2:6, 9, 12, 15, 19). *"The glory of the LORD* [and] *the splendor of our God"* (Isa. 35:2) will be seen in the healing of blind eyes, the opening of deaf ears, the healing of paralytics and mute tongues (Isa. 35:5). As the blind see, the deaf hear, paralytics walk, and mute tongues shout for joy, these miracles will become "convincing proofs" (Acts1:3) that Jesus is alive and the only true Redeemer—and many will believe!

Many diseases and physical disorders (some unique to the end-time and therefore very frightening) for which there are no medical cures, things impossible with man, will be healed as manifestations of God's glory and power. These miracles will be visible signs and testimonies to the world about the true God. Miracles will be so notable that the evil side will be compelled to try to imitate them with counterfeits. Counterfeits appear only when the genuine is in widespread public awareness.

In the most evil time in history, believers who are loyal disciples will know Jesus intimately and be full of the Holy Spirit and His power. Jesus' Bride then will be a worshiping and praying army, anointed with power to release miracles, signs, and wonders like those during the time of the Old Testament exodus and the New Testament apostles.

During the end-time conflict, as persecution increases globally against Christians, there will be also an increase of God's activity on behalf of those He loves. Compassion and love in God's heart for His people will fuel both the fire in His eyes for His Bride and the fire of His wrath against Satan.

Some of God's greatest signs in the end-time will be in the form of judgments. During the OT exodus, Psalm 135:9 says: *"He sent his signs and wonders into your midst, Egypt, against Pharaoh and all his servants."* Likewise, in the end-time the Book of Revelation tells us about two God-appointed prophets who will testify with signs and wonders about Jesus in Jerusalem and the Middle East with the whole world watching (11:10).

> *These men have power to shut up the sky so that it will not rain during the time they are prophesying [the Elijah anointing]; and they have power to turn the waters into blood and to strike the earth with every kind of plague [the Moses anointing] as often as they want* (Rev. 11:6).

Then it will be true, as never before, that *"those living far away fear your wonders"* (Psa. 65:8a). The majority of the world's inhabitants will be resistant, hardened and belligerent to God's supernatural signs and judgments; others, however, will be softened and awed by God's signs and be saved (Joel 2:32; Rev. 7:9, 14; 11:13). The coming great revival will indeed be a time of great signs and mighty wonders that testify to the Most High God and the eternality of His kingdom (cf., Dan. 4:2–3).

6. Great Global Harvest

The Bible makes numerous prophetic statements that point to an enormous end-time harvest of salvation that will be gathered in every part of the world among all nations. Consistent with Joel's prophecy of a global outpouring at the very end is the prophecy in Revelation 7:9, 14 about a massive worldwide harvest involving all nations, tribes, people and tongues *during* the time of great trouble in the earth.

Present twenty-first century intercessory prayer for revival by an unprecedented multitude of intercessors worldwide will result in an unprecedented worldwide spiritual harvest that will be incomprehensively great numerically. Every nation, every tribe, and every people and language group on the earth (Rev. 7:9) will contribute to this innumerably great harvest at the end of the age.

Historically, great harvests of salvation since AD 1500 have always occurred in the context of great revivals. Logically and exegetically, the final great harvest will be the result of the coming great revival and spiritual awakening.

Biblical Evidence

Does biblical evidence contradict or support an end-time revival of enormous consequence? The following biblical evidence clearly points to a last revival at the end of history before Christ returns that is both global and statistically great.

The coming great global outpouring of the Spirit about which Joel 2 prophesies, and the final end-time harvest that Scripture describes in Revelation 7, both occur at the end-time and are inter-related. John aptly describes for us a globally great harvest which he saw in a vision:

> *After this I looked and there before me was a great multitude that no one could count, from every nation, tribe, people and language, standing before the throne and in front of the Lamb. They were wearing white robes and were holding palm branches in their hands* (Rev. 7:9, emphasis added).

Amos also prophesies about this future spiritual harvest in prophetic terms as an exceedingly abundant natural harvest. The main point of Amos' prophecy is the vastness of the harvest:

> *"The days are coming," declares the LORD, "when the reaper will be overtaken by the plowman and the planter by the one treading grapes. New wine will drip from the mountains and flow from all the hills"* (Amos 9:13).

Jesus predicted in Matthew 13:24–30, 36–40 that both the wheat (the righteous) and the tares (the ungodly) will become fully ripe in the end-time. Similarly, in Revelation 14:14–19, John describes a great eschatological double harvest. John's description of the first harvest scene in Revelation 14 is a harvest of precious grain (14:14–16), representing the coming great revival with its end-time harvest of salvation (cf., Rev 7:9, 14) at a time when the earth is on the threshold of its greatest judgment (cf., 16:12–16; 19:11–21).

John's second scene in Revelation 14 is a harvest of grapes (14:17–20) that are gathered into the winepress of God's wrath. This harvest of grapes represents a harvest of God's judgment at a time of an unprecedented outpouring of God's wrath upon the earth (Rev. 15–16). His wrath is against those who follow the beast (i.e., antichrist—Rev. 13) in the final rebellion. Heaven's angels are active participants in these two final harvests as Revelation 14:14–20 makes clear.

The end-time harvest of salvation, like the end-time harvest of God's wrath, will be somewhat short in duration. For believers it will require great courage and enormous sacrifice of life during a time of unprecedented signs and wonders on the one hand, and intense persecution and martyrdom on the other hand. The final salvation harvest "will be the most far-reaching acceptance of the gospel this world has ever seen."[7]

The final great revival and salvation harvest are both directly associated with the return of Jesus Christ. Consider two important things about the final harvest. First, the coming great salvation harvest (like the final revival itself) will occur when the Lord's return is near (Joel 2:30–31; Rev. 14:14–16). The return of the Lord Jesus is awaiting this great spiritual revolution near the end of the age.

Second, God is like the farmer in James 5:7 who patiently waits for the full maturation of the "valuable" harvest because He doesn't want "anyone to perish, but everyone to come to repentance" (2 Pet. 3:9). Every day that the Lord Jesus lingers before returning is a summons for the church to earnestly intercede for the great coming revival and salvation harvest, and to prepare herself for completing the great commission (Matt. 24:14; 28:18).

Numerically Great

Since the coming great eschatological outpouring (revival) about which Joel 2 prophesies and the coming final harvest that John describes in Revelation 7, both occur at the end-time, they are necessarily inter-related. Likewise, since the great harvest that John describes in Revelation 7:9 and the abundant harvest that Amos describes in Amos 9:13–14 are both eschatological, they too are inter-related.

The harvest that John saw in a vision was not only globally great but numerically great: *After this I looked and there before me was **a great multitude that no one could count**, from every nation, tribe, people and language. . .* (Rev. 7:9, emphasis added).

The harvest *"from every nation [and] tribe"* that John saw was so vast that no one could statistically keep count of it (Rev. 7:9). Likewise, the abundant harvest about which Amos prophesied (cf. Amos 9:13) was so vast in its abundance that the harvesters had great difficulty finishing their task. The biblical prophecies about a "double portion" and a "hundred fold" fruitfulness (about which both the Old Testament and the New Testament speak) will happen on every continent at this time.

A world population study officially released by the United Nations reveals the following dramatic population increase:

AD 1   300 million people (when Jesus was on the earth)

AD 1000 310 million people (net increase of only 10 million in 1,000 years)

AD 1500 500 million people (time of the Protestant Reformation)

AD 1900 1.5 billion people (net increase of 1 billion in only 400 years)

AD 2000 6.25 billion (net increase 5 billion in only 100 years)

AD 2025 8.5 billion projected people (in only 25 years)

The implications of this for the Spirit-empowered church globally are sobering. It is now possible for more people to be saved in the twenty-first century than in all previous centuries combined.

Based on the pattern of previous historic revivals, the massive final harvest of salvation will come predominantly from *three broad categories of people:* (1) youth and young adults, (2) the poor of the world, and (3) those who are caught in the web of false religions.

On the one hand, these three categories represent the largest portion of the world's population. On the other hand, they are the ones historically who are most responsive to the gospel when presented with the truth and evidence of Jesus in the context of powerful revival. Obviously, the impact will include other categories of people, but these three categories will be primary and should be targeted in prayer.

The revived church's responsibility will be not only to reap the harvest, but also to disciple new believers for the Lord Jesus Christ. God the Father promised His Son the nations as His inheritance (Psa. 2:7–8). Jesus' great commissioning instruction to the church is to go in His authority to *make disciples of all nations, baptizing them . . . and teaching them to obey everything I have commanded you. And surely I am with you always,* **to the very end of the age** [the last salvation harvest] (Matt. 28:18–20, emphasis added). The coming great revival and harvest is about Jesus' rightful inheritance—the nations!

7. Great Transformation

Hebrews 2:3–4 speaks of *"great salvation"* . . . *"which was first announced by the Lord, [and] was confirmed to us by those who heard him. God also testified to it by signs, wonders and various miracles, and gifts of the Holy Spirit distributed according to his will."*

The "great salvation" that Jesus and the early church proclaimed involved the full victory of the cross and the full scope of redemption. This "great salvation" provided victory over sin, deliverance from demonic bondage, healing—both physical and emotional, and the gifts of the Holy Spirit.

Moreover, this "great salvation" speaks of the broad scope of redemption and thus encompasses the activity of God in great transformation. Supernatural transformation today among the nations is a more extensive expression of God's redemptive intention than the church has seen thus far in her history.

Transforming revival is a strategic part of God's plan for bringing redemption to fullness before Jesus returns. Transformation during the coming great revival will encompass not only the transformation of individuals, marriages and families, but the collective transformation of entire congregations and communities during the powerful manifestations of God's presence and power in geographical regions.

When God's transforming presence has been welcomed by a prepared people, the spiritual atmosphere will become a "canopy" of favor, blessing and protection. *"Now My eyes will be open and My ears attentive to the prayers offered in this place"* (2 Chron. 7:15). These communities will become places of refuge in the days of great trouble and beacons of light and hope in the increasing darkness and chaos.

In the coming great revival, phenomenal ecological miracles will appear, even as vast ecological judgments are occurring worldwide. The transformational miracles of land we are witnessing today are an eschatological precursor of the approaching fullness of redemption when Christ returns to transform the whole earth into an arena for His glory (Habakkuk 2:14, Isaiah 35; Isaiah 65:17-18, Rev. 21:22-24). The new dimension of revival in the 21st century includes the transformation of the land itself. How important will transformation of land be for believers in times of famine and great food shortage!

The transformational dimension of the coming revival will be an eschatological sign that cannot be ignored and will signal that the full manifestation of God's glory and redemption are at hand. The full victory of the cross will be on display in the great spiritual harvest among the nations.

Described another way, a great tsunami of revival, salvation, healing, deliverance from demons and transformation of people, communities and land will penetrate the nations. It will be a time when the heavens will be open, both for salvation and judgment, and God's mighty acts and deeds will be on a scale never before seen on the earth.

8. Great Bridal Transformation

The Holy Spirit is presently preparing the church for both her greatest revival and her greatest pressure ever in church history. The Western church is not ready for either great revival or great pressure! The church in decadent Western cultures is seriously tainted and defiled by her compromise with the spirit of the world and is busy justifying her sin by a doctrine of cheap grace.

Jesus is coming for a healthy, radiant, and transformed Bride. He is not returning for a self-centered, compromised church infiltrated by the spirit of the age. God is not finished with His church.

The coming great revival will play a big role in the final restoration and preparation of the Bride for the Bridegroom. Revival will ready the church as the people of God to live in intimacy with Christ, in oneness with the Holy Spirit, and in agreement with the core values of God's kingdom.

When Jesus—the Bridegroom—appears, the prepared Bride will be like the five virgins who were prepared and waiting expectantly for His arrival (Matt. 25:1–13). The prepared Bride will be *radiant. . . , without stain or wrinkle or any other blemish, but holy and blameless* (Eph. 5:–27). The Bible testifies that the radiant Bride will have "made herself ready" for the Bridegroom (Rev. 19:7) and will agree as one voice with the Spirit preceding Jesus' return (Rev. 22:12–15, 17).

The church corporately will not make this journey to full maturity and readiness (Eph. 4:13) without the catalyst of revival and troubled times. Without the intervention of revival and the turmoil of great trouble, the Western church will continue comfortably in her present status quo of materialism and compromise.

For this purpose, God's judgment will begin with "the household of God" (1 Pet. 4:17). Before the final trumpet sounds, Jesus will take His stand in the congregation of His people (Psa. 82:1 NASB) as the Bridegroom Judge. He will come in righteous jealousy for His beloved and as the "refiner's fire" to purify His people, like gold and silver are purified by fire.

When the Bride repents of her unfaithfulness and returns to her first love, the Refiner will mercifully relent and come in His manifest presence to revive and transform His church (cf., Acts 3:19). The purging fires of revival, and of God's judgments in the earth, will bring His people into the true beauty of holiness.

There will be two fully developed parallel tracks at the end: the Bride of Christ in purity (Rev. 19) and the boastful harlot (ecumenical religion) brazen in her impurity (Rev. 17, 18). The purifying fires of the Bride will include great trouble, persecution, and martyrdom. A massive harvest of true salvation and radical disciples will occur in contrast to and in conflict with a hostile global-ecumenical-religious movement that is politically correct and fully aligned with the spirit of the world. In the end, there will be both the full unveiling of evil and the full unveiling of God's glory in the Bride (Eph. 3:21).

9. Great Spiritual Awakening in Israel

John, in Revelation 7:9 describes the great salvation harvest at the end-time as involving *"every nation [and] tribe." **Every nation** would necessarily include the nation of Israel. This is indicated also in the following two Old Testament prophecies:

- Joel 2:32 states: *And everyone who calls on the name of the LORD will be saved; for on Mount Zion and in Jerusalem there will be deliverance.* Notice the great outpouring of the Spirit "on all people" (Joel 2:28) includes "Mount Zion" and "Jerusalem" (Joel 2:32).

- Amos 9:13–14, also prophetically describes the great harvest as including Israel: *"The days are coming,"* declares the LORD, *"when the reaper will be overtaken by the plowman and the planter by the one treading grapes. New wine will drip from the mountains and flow from all the hills. I will bring back my exiled people Israel; they will rebuild the ruined cities and live in them* (emphasis added).

Both the above passages are eschatological and explicitly include Israel in the final harvest. The coming great revival and spiritual harvest at the end of the age will emphatically include Israel as Romans 11:12–27 also makes clear.

Israel will not be left out! Because of Israel's hardened heart and unbelief about Yeshua (Jesus) after His death, resurrection, ascension and the church's apostolic witness with signs and wonders, *"God gave them a spirit of stupor"* (Rom. 11:8). But Israel's spiritual stupor or veil and her contemporary spiritual dullness is destined to be lifted! Global revival and spiritual awakening will reach Israel near the close of the age, resulting in her salvation and preparing the way for Jesus' second coming.

Romans 11:12 speaks of Israel's "fullness" redemptively and her great future salvation in relation to great salvation among the Gentiles—i.e., the nations.

> *If their [Israel's] transgression means riches for the world, . . .*
> *how much greater riches will their fullness bring!* (Rom. 11:12).

Using the olive tree analogy to represent salvation history, Paul states that because of unbelief Israel was (like branches), cut off from the tree of salvation (Rom. 11:20). But he adds:

> *And if they [Israelites] do not persist in unbelief, they will be*
> *grafted in, for God is able to graft them in again. After all, if*
> *you [saved Gentiles]were cut out of an olive tree that is wild by*
> *nature, and contrary to nature were grafted into a cultivated*
> *olive tree [tree of salvation], how much more readily will these,*
> *the natural branches* [Israel], *be grafted into their own olive*
> *tree* (Rom. 11:23–24)!

Paul indicates that the time is coming when Israel will experience a national revival and as a result will be grafted back into the tree of salvation. He calls this collective grafting back into the olive tree, Israel's "fullness" redemptively (Rom. 11:12). When will this occur? The coming great revival will be the catalyst! Only then will salvation history approach its fullness and completeness.

Romans 11:26 speaks of Israel's "fullness" (Rom. 11:12) in terms of "all Israel" being saved:

> *Israel has experienced a hardening in part until the full number*
> *of the Gentiles has come in. And so **all Israel** will be saved, as*
> *it is written: 'The deliverer will come from Zion; he will turn*
> *godlessness away from Jacob. And this is my covenant with*
> *them when I take away their sins'* (Rom. 11:25b–27, emphasis
> added).

This passage has long puzzled biblical scholars, evidenced by their many different interpretations of its meaning. One thing is clear, "all Israel" is not presently saved. The present nation of Israel is a secular state, mostly comprised of Jews who are not religious, many are atheists, and only 1% believes in Yeshua as their Messiah. When will the "fullness" of their salvation occur as spoken of in Romans 11:12, 26? Biblical prophesies like Ezekiel 20:42–44, Jeremiah 31:34, and Romans 11:26 point to a revival of repentance and acceptance of the Messiah (Yeshua) in Israel on a grand scale (cf., Jer. 31:27–34; 32:37–33:26; Ezek. 16:60–63; 37:1–28; Amos 9:11–15; Rev. 7:1–17).

The sequence seems to be a great global revival (primarily Gentiles) that also reaches and impacts Israel, resulting in an unprecedented harvest and revival in Israel. Possibly the revival in Israel will (in turn) help fuel the final stage of the global revival so that it reaches its fullest measure and culmination (cf., Joel 2:23–27; Hos. 6:1–3, 11; Rom. 11:12).

God's covenant promise to Abraham intricately involved the Promise Land for him and his descendants, even the whole nation of Israel. This land was to be Israel's inheritance forever (Deut. 4:21, 38; 12:9; 15:4; 19:10; 20:16; 21:23; 24:4; 25:19; 26:1).

In the Old Testament, whenever Israel turned from God to idolatry—war, calamity, and loss of the land would occur. Whenever they renewed their covenant and had a revival of faith and faithfulness in Israel, their land would be restored. In Jeremiah 33:26, Yahweh renews His pledge to restore the land as Israel's inheritance and says this covenant promise is as certain as day and night (Jer. 33:20, 25).

Paul in Romans 11:11–32 picks up this theme of God's everlasting covenant with Israel that will yet be fully realized. When Paul writes, *"And so all Israel will be saved"* (Rom. 11:26), it is in keeping with Isaiah 27:9 and 59:20–21. Walter Kaiser comments that Romans 11:26 doesn't say that every Israelite will experience salvation (Rom. 9:6, 27), but that Israel collectively (as a nation) will "experience the blessing and joy of God spiritually, materially, geographically, and politically."[8] Salvation of Israel and her land are not only promised by God, but also are to be contended for by the church in intercession on Israel's behalf until God's covenant promise and purposes are fully realized.

Worship and intercession presently rises to the throne of God daily in various houses of prayer throughout the land of Israel. As the church, we must stand in agreement with God's plans for Israel, her people and the Promised Land. The coming great revival will both reach and impact Israel with great awakening, great salvation, and ultimately great national transformation when Jesus returns in their hour of greatest crisis.

10. Great Redemptive Fullness

The "fullness" promises in the New Testament will begin to converge with the coming great revival. This ultimate revival will be the catalyst for redemptive fullness at the end of this age. For the past 500 years, God has used historic revivals for restoring the church and bringing redemption to its next stage of development. In keeping with this pattern, the coming revival will be God's appointed means for bringing the church and redemption to their appointed fullness and completion before the Lord Jesus Christ returns.

Three times Paul speaks of fullness in Ephesians. First, he refers to the church—Christ's body—as *"the fullness of him who fills everything in every way"* (Eph. 1:23). Second, Paul prays that believers *"may be filled to the measure of all the fullness of God"* (Eph. 3:19). Third, Paul states that God gave gifted leaders— i.e., apostles, prophets, evangelists, pastors, and teachers—so that the body of Christ may be built up, until we *"become mature, attaining to the whole measure of the fullness of Christ"* (Eph. 4:13). In all three of these profound references, Paul is aspiring to see the church come to a place of fullness that we presently have not realized.

The coming great revival will bring the outworking of redemption to an unprecedented fullness before Christ returns.

But God will not do so apart from His people contending in faith and prayer for fullness. Before the church is a mature bride, the church must contend for "the whole measure of the fullness of Christ" (Eph. 4:13). Before we see transformed cities and the salvation remnant among nations as the inheritance of Christ, the church must contend in prayer and faith for these things.

God has promised a revival from heaven that will touch "all people" (Joel 2:28), result in the salvation of "all Israel" (Rom. 11:26), and ultimately lead to the redemption of "all creation" (Rom. 8:22). Still God requires His people to partner with Him in praying and faith for the fullness of these vast promises.

In the progression of redemptive and revival history, we are moving in the direction of fullness. Proverbs 4:18 (NASB) states that redemptive progression is "like the light of dawn, that shines brighter and brighter until the full day." Jesus taught us to pray for His Kingdom to come now and His will to be done on earth now.

We cannot be honest with Scripture and relegate the "fullness" promises to "the age to come" when the context of the Scriptural promises place them squarely in "this age." We tend to mentally file God's promises of redemptive fullness to the second coming simply because we haven't seen evidence of fullness in this age. But God never does everything all at once! Redemptive history has unfolded progressively until now; in the twenty-first century we are seeing glimpses of "first fruit" fullness.

God's *future* kingdom when Jesus returns and His kingdom fully comes to the earth even now breaks into the present through revival and His redemptive actions! How much of God and His kingdom can we experience this side of Jesus' second coming? Who knows for sure, but it is safe to say we can see a far greater measure of it than we have seen so far.

Contemporary supernatural transformation in places like Almolonga (Guatemala) and in Fiji and other South Pacific islands, is surely an eschatological sign of the approaching fullness of redemption when Christ returns to transform the whole earth into an arena for His glory (cf., Isa 65:17-25).

The coming great revival among all nations will be the forerunner of fullness, the first fruits of the transformation of people, nations, and land that will occur when Jesus returns to reign on the earth for a thousand years. Not only will His government be established fully, but also we will see the full restoration and transformation of every sphere of life and land. In the meantime, Jesus is seeking to reconcile all things in Himself through the blood of His cross (Col. 1:19–20).

Conclusion

Circumstances are accelerating globally that are moving us toward the final great clash between light and darkness. The coming great revival will be a critical part of this catastrophic climax. The prince of darkness is aggressively implementing his sinister plans for the final great rebellion against God and His Christ and the Bride. But God is also quickening the pace of implementing His strategy for transforming the Bride and for reaping the spiritual harvest among the nations.

The end-time revival will restore Jesus' *rightful place* as the Head of His Body, the church. God is maturing the church so that she can grow up into the Head, Christ Jesus, and thereby attain to the whole measure of the fullness of Christ in full agreement with the Holy Spirit (Eph. 4:13, 15–16).

The end-time revival will also enable Jesus' *rightful relationship* with His prepared Bride to be realized. The Father will look at the earth, see that the Bride has made herself ready (Rev. 19:7), and will then say to the Son at His right hand: "the time is full for You to return to earth!"

When Jesus returns to the earth, breaking through with His presence and power, He will receive the "title deed" to the earth, fulfill every promise of redemption and rid the earth of the evil one. The nations will then come under the rule of Jesus as King of all the earth and the government will rest squarely on His shoulders (Isa. 9:6–7). The Bride will reign with Him forever and ever (Rev 21:2, 22:5). And the earth—the land itself—will be fully transformed (Is. 35:1–10; 65:17–25).

In light of the present hour and the anticipation of the coming revival, we must prepare ourselves for the approaching glory and presence of God. It is time to get our personal lives, our families, our congregations and communities focused on the Father's business. Now is the time to deal decisively with all compromise and sin issues. We must be ruthless with anything in our lives which grieves the Holy Spirit or hinders Him from partnering with us in these important days.

As God's people worldwide yearn and pray as never before for the spiritual realities that are approaching, God will be faithful to bring all redemption to its promised fullness. Then the Spirit and the Bride will say together in perfect agreement, "Come!" (Rev. 22:17), and the King of Glory will come!

End Notes

Chapter 1

1   Billy Graham, "The King Is Coming" in *Let The Earth Hear His Voice: Official Reference Volume for the International Congress on World Evangelism*, Lausanne, Switzerland, ed. J.D. Douglas (Minneapolis: World Wide Publications, 1975), 1466 (emphasis is added*).*

Chapter 2

1   Owen Murphy and John Wesley Adams, *The Fire of God's Presence: Powerful Lessons from the Hebrides Revival, 2nd Edition* (Kansas City: Ambassadors Press, 2004), 13.

2   Robert Coleman "Foreword" in Malcolm McDow and Alvin L. Reid, *Firefall: How God Has Shaped History through Revivals* (Nashville: Broadman & Holman Publishers, 1997), vii.

3   J. Edwin Orr, Lecture (Waco, Tx: Baylor University, 1975).

4   Wesley L. Duewel, *Revival Fire* (Grand Rapids: Zondervan Publishing House, 1995), 11.

5   J. Edwin Orr, *The Fervent Prayer: The Worldwide Impact of the Great Awakening of 1858* (Chicago: Moody Press, 1974), vii.

6   Malcolm McDow and Alvin L. Reid, *Firefall: How God Has Shaped History through Revivals* (Nashville: Broadman & Holman Publishers, 1997), 3.

7   George Otis, Jr., teaching DVD from Brazil conference May, 2007.(Lynwood, Wash: The Sentinel Group).

8   Frank Bartleman, *Azusa Street: An Eyewitness Account* (Plainfield, N.J.: Bridge-Logos Publishing, 1980), 58-60. Originally published as *How Pentecost Came to Los Angeles: As It Was In the Beginning, Old Azusa Mission—From My Diary* (Los Angeles: F. Bartleman Publisher, 1925).

Chapter 3

1   Arthur Wallis, *Revival: Rain From Heaven* (Old Tappan, NJ: Fleming H. Revell, 1985), 13 (emphasis added).

2   Earle E. Cairns, Christianity through the Centuries: A History of the Christian Church, 3rd edition (Grand Rapids: Zondervan Publishing House, 1996) 323-330.

3   Russell D. Moore,*God, the Gospel, and Glenn Beck.* Published Sunday, August 29th, 2010. *Moore to the Point*, www.russellmoore.com.

4   James Burns, *Revivals: Their Laws and Leaders* (Grand Rapids: Baker Book House, 1960), original (London: Hodder and Stoughton, 1909), 70.

5   Andrew Woolsey, *Duncan Campbell—A Biography: The Sound of Battle* (London: Hodder and Stoughton [for] the Faith Mission, 1974) 113.
6   Murphy and Adams, *The Fire of God's Presence*, 31.
7   Ibid.
8   Ibid.
9   Duewel, *Revival Fire*, 11.
10 Ibid., 13
11 Orr, J. Edwin. "The Role of Prayer in Spiritual Awakening". DVD Campus Crusade for Christ, 2006. (Randolph Productions, Irvine, CA).
12 Ibid.
13 Duewel, "Will You Open the Door?" *Holiness Digest* (Spring 1977), 15.
14 Charles Grandison Finney, *Memoirs of Rev. Charles G. Finney: The American Evangelist* (New York: Fleming H. Revell Company, 1876) 65.
15 Arthur Wallis, *Revival:The Rain from Heaven* (Fleming H. Revell Company: Power Books, 1979) 73.

Chapter 4

1   McDow & Reid, *Firefall*, 184.
2   Ibid.
3   William Wilberforce, *William Wilberforce: Greatest Works* (Alachua, FL: Bridge-Logos, 2007), 33–40.
4   Orr, *The Fervent Prayer*, 14–19.
5   Murphy and Adams, *The Fire of God's Presence*, 15.
6   Timothy L. Smith, *Revivalism & Social Reform: American Protestantism on the Eve of the Civil War* (New York: Harper and Row, 1965, originally published by New York: Abingdon Press, 1957).
7   Ibid.
8   Robert J. Morgan, "Devotional for June 16," *On This Day:365 Amazing and Inspiring Stories About Saints, Martyrs and Heroes* (Nashville: Thomas Nelson Inc, 1997).
9   Minnie L. Carpenter, *William Booth: Founder of the Salvation Army,* (London: Epworth Press, 1957) also online: www1.salvationarmy.org/heritage.nsf/AllSubCategories? OpenView&RestrictToCategory =William_Booth&main=People, 2003.
10 Roy Hattersley, *Blood and Fire: The Story of William and Catherine Booth and the Salvation Army* (New York: Doubleday, 1999), jacket cover.
11 Carpenter, *William Booth* online.
12 Robert L. Bradshaw, *Bending the Church to Save the World: The Welsh Revival of 1904.* www.robibrad.demon.co.uk/pdf/revival.pdf, (1995).
13 Murphy and Adams, *The Fire of God's Presence*, 16.
14 Luis Lugo, "The Pew Forum on Religion & Public Life," *Historical Overview of Pentecostalism in Brazil.*,Online http://pewforum.org/Christian/ Evangelical-Protestant-Churches/Historical-Overview-of-Pentecostalism-in-

Brazil.aspx (October 5, 2006). Origins and Growth, bullet 6.

15　Raul Zibechi, "Brazzil: Since 1989 Trying to Understand Brazil", *How Brazil Benefits from Being World's Most Pentecostal Country*. Online: www.brazzil.com/articles/197-october-2008/10120-how-brazil-benefits-from-being-worlds-most-pentecostal-country.html (October 15, 2008) paragraph 5.

16　John Marcom Jr., "The Fire Down South," *Forbes* (October 15, 1990), 64.

17　Ibid, 71.

18　Murphy, and Adams, *The Fire of God's Presence*, 75–76.

19　Duncan Campbell, *The Price and Power of Revival: Lessons from the Hebrides Awakening* (Edinburgh: The Faith Mission, n.d.), 51.

20　Andrew Woolsey, *Duncan Campbell: A Biography: The Sound of Battle* (London: Hodder and Stoughton [for] the Faith Mission, 1974), 113.

Chapter 5

1　Bruce Atkinson, *Land of Hope and Glory: British Revival Through the Ages*. (London: Dovewell Publications, 2003), 41–56.

2　Duewel, *Revival Fire*, 43.

3　John Greenfield, *Power from On High: The Story of the Great Moravian Revival of 1727* (Fort Washington, PA: Christian Literature Crusade, 1950).

4　William Wilberforce, p. 38

5　Ibid, pgs 39-40

6　Roberts Liardon, *God's Generals: Why They Succeeded and Why Some Failed* (Tulsa: Albury Publishing, 1996), 72

7　Ibid., 164.

8　G. Leibholz, "Memoir," in Dietrich Bonhoeffer, *The Cost of Discipleship*, trans. Edwin H. Robertson and John Bowden (New York: Harbor & Row, 1963), 11–35.

9　Eberhard Bethge, "Editors forward," *Letters and Papers from Prison* by Dietrich Bonhoeffer (London: S.C.M. Press, 1953), pgs 7-11.

10　Leibholz, "Memoir" in Bonhoeffer, *The Cost of Discipleship*, 14.

11　Ibid., 21.

12　Ibid., 23.

Chapter 6

1　McDow and Reid, *Firefall*, 170.

2　Ibid., 175.

3　Cf. J. Edwin Orr, *Campus Aflame* (Glendale, CA: Regal Books, 1971), 1–235; McDow & Reid, *Firefall*, 208–220, 235–239, 247–249.

4　Bernard Bailyn, *The Ideological Origins of the American Revolution* (Cambridge, MA: Harvard University Press, 1967), I, 66.

5   Bartleman, *Azusa Street*, 182–184.
6   Vinson Synan, *The Century of the Holy Spirit:100 years of Pentecostal and charismatic renewal, 1901-2001* (Nashville: Thomas Nelson , 2001).
7   Harvey Cox, *Fire From Heaven: The Rise of Pentecostal Spirituality and the Reshaping of Religion in the Twenty-First Century* (Reading, Mass.: Addison-Wesley, 1995), 65.

Chapter 7

1. *Transformations I: A Documentary*, film by The Sentinel Group, 1999. To order, see the Sentinel Group Web site: http://sentinelgroup.org/dvds.asp.
2   See DVDs produced by George Otis, Jr., Founder and President of the Sentinel Group, documenting supernaturally transformed communities and even transformed land (ecological miracles) that reveal a powerful testimony of God's glory among the nations. You may purchase these documentary DVDs at www.fusionministry.com

Chapter 8

1   George Otis, Jr., *Informed Intercession* (Grand Rapids, MI: Baker Book House, 1990?) , p. 55.
2   http://glowtorch.org/JourneytoTransformation/WhatDoesTransformationLookLike
3   *The Quickening film by The Sentinel Group, 2003. To order, see the Sentinel Group Web site: http://sentinelgroup.org/dvds.asp.*
4   *http://glowtorch.org/JourneytoTransformation/WhatDoesTransformationLookLike.*

Chapter 10

1   Orr, "The Role of Prayer in Spiritual Awakening."
2   Andrew Murray, *With Christ in the School of Prayer* (Westwood, NJ: Spire Books, 1965), 85.
3   John Telford, *The Life of John Wesley* (New York: Hunt & Eaton, n.d.), 117.
4   Orr, J. Edwin. "The Role of Prayer in Spiritual Awakening". DVD Campus Crusade for Christ, 2006. (Randolph Productions, Irvine, CA).
5   *Angels (and Demons): What Do we Really Know About Them?* Peter J. Kreeft. 1995. Ignitius Press.
6   For a vivid description of the Hebrides Revival and its enduring principles, see *The Fire of God's Presence* by Murphy and Adams (available at www.fusionministry.com).
7   Merrill F. Unger, "Humility," *New Unger's Bible Dictionary,* (Chicago,

IL: Moody Publishers, 1988).

8   http://glowtorch.org/FireQuest/OmkoiThailand/tabid/2676/Default.aspx

9   Rhonda Hughey, *Desperate for His Presence* (Minneapolis, MN: Bethany House Publishers, 2004), p. 140

10   Ibid p. 143

Chapter 11

1   Dietrich Bonhoeffer, *The Cost of Discipleship*, p. 45.

2   C. Peter Wagner, *Hard-Core Idolatry: Facing the Facts* (Colorado Springs: Wagner Publications, 1999, 2001) p. 12.

3   American Religious Identification Survey 2001, (The Barna Research Group, 2004)

4   *World Almanac.* (New York: Press Publishing Co., 2004, 2003, 2000).

5   Donald C. Stamps and John Wesley Adams (eds.), "Standards of Sexual Morality," *Life in the Spirit Study Bible* (Grand Rapids, MI: Zondervan, 1991; 2003), pp. 1970-71.

6   "Current Statistics," Internet, http://www.nationalcoalition.org/

7   "'Safe Sex' for the Whole Nation," Editorial, *Christianity Today Online*, March 22, 2007. http://www.christianitytoday.com/ct/2007/april/18.26.html.

8   Lou Engle, "40 Days for 40 Years: Calling America to a 40-day Fast," a message delivered at Forerunner Christian Fellowship (Kansas City, Missouri) on May 20th, 2007.

9   Pastor's Family Bulletin, Focus on the Family, March 2000.

10   The two primary sources of U.S. abortion statistics are Centers for Disease Control and Alan Guttmacher Institute.

11   Vuniani Nakauyaca and Walo Ani, *Healing the Land Manual* (Toowoomba city Church, 2007)

12   For the testimony of a pastor who has transitioned his church from program-driven to presence-based, see Lonnie Parton's book, Desperate People in Desperate Times (Cedar Rapids, IA: Arrow Press, 2010), 80 pages.

Chapter 12

1   Robert E. Coleman, The Coming World Revival (Wheaton, IL: Crossway, 1995); article by Coleman, "The Coming World Revival," in Perspectives on the World Christian Movement, eds. Ralph D. Winter and Steve Hawthorne.

2   Robert E. Coleman, The Coming World Revival, p. 150.

3   Collin Hansen, "The Case for Christendom," *Christianity Today* Magazine (August 24, 2009).

4   Mike Bickle with Brian Kim, 7 Commitments of a Forerunner (Kansas
     City, MO: Forerunner Press, 2010)
5   Bickle, 7 Commitments of a Forerunner, p. 6.
6   Cf. Robert E. Coleman, The Coming World Revival, p. 153.
7   Robert E. Coleman, The Coming World Revival, p. 156.
8   Walter C. Kaiser, Jr., "The Promised Land: A Biblical-Historical View,"
     Bibliotheca Sacra 138:552 (October 1981), p. 310.

Select Annotated Revival Bibliography

Revivalists in Church History Reference Works

Burgess, Stanley, and McGee, Gary (eds.). *Dictionary of Pentecostal and Charismatic Movements.* Grand Rapids: Zondervan, 1988. An excellent source of information on the Pentecostal and Charismatic revivals and the leaders of these movements.

Curtis, A. Kenneth; Lang, J. Stephen; Petersen, Randy. *The 100 Most Important Events in Christian*

History. Grand Rapids: Fleming H. Revell, 1991. Rich and succinct source of information on great revival leaders.

Douglas, J. D. (Gen. Ed.). *The New International Dictionary of the Christian Church.* Grand Rapids: Zondervan, 1974. Brief summaries.

The Journal of John Wesley (Letters, Sermons, Journals) (originally 26 vols).

Available at Christian Classics Ethereal Library online at http://www. ccel.org

The Journals or Writings of others like George Whitefield, Jonathan Edwards, Charles G. Finney and many others are available free online.

Eyewitness Accounts of Revival

Bartleman, Frank. *Azusa Street.* Plainfield, NJ: Logos 1980. The foremost eyewitness account by a leader who participated in this revival.

Campbell, Duncan. *God's Standard.* Fort Washington, PA: Christian Literature Crusade, 1967. By God's chosen vessel in the Hebrides Revival of 1949-1952.

Coleman, Robert E. (ed.). *One Divine Moment*. Westwood, NJ: Fleming
    H. Revels, 1970. Reflections by firsthand witnesses of the 1970 cam-
    pus revival at Asbury College in Kentucky.

Edwards, Jonathan. *On Revival*. Carlisle, PA: Banner of Truth, 1984 (re-
    print). This compiles Edwards' three famous treatises on revival: "A
    Narrative of Surprising Conversions;" "The Distinguishing Marks
    of the Work of the Spirit of God;" and "An Account of the Revival of
    Religion in Northhampton 1740-1742."

Finney, Charles G. *Lectures on Revival*. Minneapolis: Bethany House,
    1988 (reprint). These 22 revival lectures (1843) by America's foremost
    revivalist discuss the practical meaning of revival and evangelism.
    Though dated and controversial, this book is a classic that has ex-
    erted more influence in the study of revival than any other work.

Jones, Brynmoor P. *Voices from the Welsh Revival 1904-1905*. Wales, UK:
    Evangelical Press of Wales, 1995. An anthology of testimonies,
    reports, and eyewitness statements from Wales' year of blessing 1904-
    1905.

Matthews, David. *I Saw the Welsh | Revival*. Chicago: Moody Press, 1951.
    This is a descriptive firsthand account of the powerful Welsh Revival
    that ushered in the 20th century and reverberated around the world.

Peckham, Colin and Mary. *Sounds from Heaven: The Revival on the Island of
    Lewis 1949-1952*. Scotland: Christian Focus, 2004. This is the only full
    length book on the Hebrides Revival by eyewitnesses other than by
    Duncan Campbell.

Penn-lewis, Mrs. Jessie. *The Awakening in Wales*. London: Marshall
    Brothers 1905. A firsthand account of the Welsh Revival in 1904.

Penn-lewis Mrs. Jessie; and Roberts, Evan. *War on the Saints*. New York:
    Thomas E. Lowe, 1973. Insights into spiritual deception and warfare
    that accompany and follow revival; dates after the Welsh Revival of
    1904.

Prime, Samuel Irenaeus. *The Power of Prayer*. New York: Charles Scrib-
    ner, 1859. An eyewitness account of the prayer meeting revival
    in 1857-58 that began on Fulton Street in New York City and then
    spread widely.

Tari, Mel; and Dudley Cliff. *Like a Mighty Wind*. Carol Stream, IL: Cre-
    ation House, 1972. An account of the miraculous events that accom-
    panied the revival in Indonesia (1960's).

Valdez, A. C. *Fire on Azusa Street*. Costa Mesa, CA: Gift Publications,
    1980. A firsthand recollection of this revival.

Warner, Wayne E. (ed.) *Revival! Touched by Pentecostal Fire: Eyewitness to Early Twentieth-Century Pentecostal Revival.* Tulsa: Harrison House, 1978. This compiles 40 interesting entries by firsthand witnesses of revival fire.

Wesley, John; Wesley, Charles; and Whitefield, George. *The Nature of Revival.* Compiled, edited, and abridged by Clare George Weakly, Jr. Minneapolis: Bethany House, 1987. Eyewitness accounts of how God moved in the great English revival of the mid 18th -century by its three most anointed participants.

Woodworth-Etter, Maria B. *Signs and Wonders God Wrought in the Ministry for Forty Years.* Indianapolis: By the author, 1916. One of the early and greatly anointed Pentecostal evangelists; her ministry is considered by some to be the most powerful yet seen in the 20th century.

Recommended Biographies of Revivalists

Bainton, Roland H. *Here I Stand: A Life of Martin Luther.* New York: New American Library, 1977.

Begbie, Harold. *The Life of William Booth.* 2 vols. London: Macmillan, 1953.

Dallimore, Arnold A. *George Whitefield: The Life and Times of the Great Evangelist of the Eighteenth- Century Revival.* 2 vols. London: Banner of Truth, 1970. A massive and definitive biography based on a careful study of primary sources.

Dallimore, Arnold A. *George Whitefield.* Wheaton, IL: Crossway Books, 1990. This paperback edition is condensed from the author's classic two-volume edition. Sherwood E. Wirt believes it is "perhaps the single-most inspiring biography published in English in the 20th century."

Douglas, W. M. *Andrew Murray and His Message.* Grand Rapids: Baker, 1981.

Drummond, Lewis A. *The Life and Ministry of Charles G. Finney.* Minneapolis: Bethany Press, 1983.

Edwards, Jonathan. *The Life and Diary of David Brainerd.* Chicago: Moody Press, 1949. This edition also contains a brief sketch of Jonathan Edwards' life. Brainerd's passionate life of prayer and devotion to God was remarkable. Mike Bickle regards this book, next to the Bible, as having the most inspirational influence on his own life during his formative years.

Finney, Charles G. *Autobiography of Charles Finney*. Minneapolis: Bethany House, 1979.

Fitt, Arthur P. *Moody Still Lives*. New York: Revell, 1936. An account of Moody's life by his son- in-law.

Graham, Billy. *Just As J Am*. San Francisco: Harper, 1997. A historically significant autobiography by the most renowned evangelist and Christian leader of the 20th century written in his later years and thus comprehensive.

Grubb, Norman. *Rees Howells, Intercessor*. Fort Washington, PA: Christian Literature Crusade,1952. Rees Howells witnessed the Welsh Revival (1904) and was an instrument in a mighty revival in Africa. His extraordinary life as an intercessor eventually had an effect on world events.

Hardman, Keith J. *Charles Grandison Finney: 1792-1875*. Grand Rapids: Baker. 1987.

Jones, Brynmoor Pierce. *An Instrument of Revival: The Complete Life of Evan Roberts 1878-1951*. South Plainfield, NJ: Bridge Publishing, 1995. The full story of his life and ministry, including the latter years of his life.

Liardon, Roberts. *God's Generals: Why They Succeeded and Why Some Failed*. Tulsa, OK: Albury Publishing, 1996. Biographical and insightful; about twelve anointed leaders in the Pentecostal and Healing Revival eras.

Lindsay, Gordon. *William Branham: A Man Sent From God*. 4th ed. Jeffersonville, IN: William Branham, 1950. Branham and Oral Roberts were the two foremost leaders in the Healing Revival of 1947-1958.

Lindsay, Gordon. *They Saw It Happen!* Dallas: Christ for the Nations, 1980 (reprint). The story of four men who were greatly used in the early part of the 20th Century outpouring of the Spirit: Charles Parham, Evan Roberts, Raymond Richey, Charles Price.

Ludwig, Charles. *Francis Asbury: God's Circuit Rider*. Milford, MI: Mott Media, 1984.

Murray, Iain, H. *Jonathan Edwards: A New Biography*. Carlisle, PA: Banner of Truth |, 1987.

Phillips, D. M. *Evan Roberts*. London: Marshall Brothers, 1923.

Pollock, John C. *George Whitefield and the Great Awakening*. Garden City, NY: Doubleday, 1972.

Pollock, John C. *John Wesley: Servant of God*. Wheaton, IL: Victor Books, 1989.

Pollock, John C. *Moody: The Biography.* New York: MacMillan, 1963.

Pollock, John C. *The Cambridge Seven: C. T. Studd and His Friends.* Leicester, England: Inter- Varsity Press, 1955, 1996.

Roberts, Oral. *The Call.* New York: Doubleday, 1972.

Steele, Ron. *Plundering Hell to Populate Heaven: The Reinhard Bonnke Story.* Melbourne, FL: Dove Christian Books, 1987.

Snyder, Howard. *The Radical Wesley: A Pattern for Revival.* Downers Grove, IL: I.V.F. Press, 1980.

Warner, Wayne E. *The Woman Evangelist: The Life and Times of Charismatic Evangelist Maria B. Woodworth-Etter.* Metuchen, NJ: The Scarecrow Press, 1986.

Weinlick, John L. *Count Zinzendorf.* New York: Abingdon, 1956.

Woodbridge, John. *Great Leaders of the Christian Church.* Chicago: Moody Press, 1988. An excellent biographical resource on revivalists and other anointed leaders of the past.

Woolsey, Andrew. *Duncan Campbell.* London: Hodder and Stoughton, 1974.

Other Noteworthy Revivalists are Savonarola, John Knox, Adam Clarke, Peter Cartwright, Phoebe Palmer, George Fox, John Lake, Smith Wigglesworth, Charles Price.

Select Resources on Revival

Boulton, Wallace, ed. *The Impact of Toronto.* Crowborough: Monarch Publications, 1995.

Burns, James. *Revivals: Their Laws and Leaders.* London: Hodder and Stoughton, 1909. This is a classic in the field of revival Literature. It was reprinted by Baker Book House in 1960, but is now out of print. It analyzes God's laws or principles operative in revival and as embodied in six revival leaders: Francis of Assisi, Savonarola, Luther, Calvin, John Knox, and John Wesley.

Bright, Bill. *The Coming Revival: America's Call to Fast, Pray and Seek God's Face.* Orlando, FL: New Life Publications, 1995. The founder and president of Campus Crusade for Christ explains how fasting and prayer cooperates with God's purpose for revival and spiritual awakening, enabling God to lift his judgment on a nation.

Campbell, Duncan. *The Price and Power of Revival: Lessons from the Hebridean Awakening.* Edinburgh: Faith Mission Publication, n.d.

Cairns, Earle E. *An Endless Line of Splendor: Revivals and Their Leaders from the Great Awakening to the Present*. Wheaton, IL: Tyndale House, 1986. A scholarly history of revivals and summary of their principles from the 18th century awakenings to the mid 20th century.

Chevreau, Guy. *Catch the Fire*. London: Marshall Pickering, 1994.

Coleman, Robert E. *The Coming World Revival*. Wheaton, IL: Crossway Books, 1995. This book explains what revival is, how it occurs, and what it will mean for the church and the world. The last chapter is on "The Hope of a Coming World Revival."

Dieter, Melvin E. *The Holiness Revival of the Nineteenth Century*. Menuchen, NJ: The Scarecrow Press, 1980.

Dixon, Patrick. *Signs of Revival*. Eastbourne: Kingsway, 1994.

Drummond, Lewis A. *The Awakening That Must Come*. Nashville: Broadman Press, 1978.

Drummond, Lewis and Betty. *Women of Awakenings: The Historic Contribution of Women to Revival Movements*. Grand Rapids: Kregel, 1997. Traces the role of twelve different women in past revivals and spiritual awakenings, including chapters on Madam Guyon, Susanna Wesley, Evangeline Booth, Amy Carmichael and Ruth Bell Graham.

Duewel, Wesley. *Revival Fire*. Grand Rapids: Zondervan, 1995.

Engle, Lou. *Digging the Wells of Revival*. Shippensburg, PA: Destiny Image, 1998.

Enroth, Ronald M., Ericson, Edward E., Jr., and Peters, C. Breckinridge. *The Jesus People*. Grand Rapids: Eerdmans, 1972. About the Jesus People Revival in the late 60s and early 70s.

Evans, Eifion. *The Welsh Revival of 1904*. Bruntirion, Wales: Evangelical Press of Wales, 1969. A careful and accurate account of the 1904 revival.

Evans, Eifion. *Revival Comes to Wales*. An account of the 1859 Welsh revival.

Fischer, Harold A. *Reviving Revivals*. Springfield, MO: Gospel Publishing House, 1950. Reviews the history of revivals and their importance.

Gee, Donald. *The Pentecostal Movement*. London: Elim Publishing Company, 1949.

Gott, Ken and Lois. *The Sunderland Refreshing*. London: Hodder & Stoughton, 1995.

Greenfield, John. *Power From On High*. Fort Washington, PA: Christian

Literature Crusade, 1950. An account of the great Moravian revival of 1727 and its influence.

Harrell, David Edwin, Jr. *All Things are Possible: The Healing and Charismatic Revivals in Modern America.* Bloomington, IN: Indiana University Press, 1975. This is the definitive history of the Healing Revival, 1947-1958; well-written and carefully documented.

Hollenweger, Walter J. *The Pentecostals.* Peabody, MA: Hendrickson Publishers, 1972.

Hughey, Rhonda. *Desperate for His Presence.* Bloomington, MN: Bethany House Publishers, 2004. A presence-based primer on transforming revival.

Kaiser, Walter C., Jr. *Quest for Renewal: Personal Revival in the Old Testament.* Chicago: Moody Press, 1986.

Kilpatrick, John. *Feast of Fire.* Pensacola, FL. 1995. Describes the Father's Day Outpouring at Brownsville Assembly of God in Pensacola, FL, and the warfare and preparation that preceded it.

Lloyd-Jones, D. Martyn. *Revival.* Westchester, IL: Crossway Books, 1987. Messages given on the 100th anniversary of the 1859 revival in Wales, containing substantial biblical, theological, and historical insights into the nature and importance of revival.

Lovelace, Richard F. *The Dynamics of Spiritual Life: An Evangelical Theology of Renewal.* Downers Grove, IL: I.V.F. Press, 1980. An excellent analysis of the theological and historical meaning of revival and spiritual renewal; contains a wealth of insightful material.

McDow, Malcolm and Reid, A. L. *Firefall: How God Has Shaped History Through Revivals.* Nashville: Broadman & Holman, 1997.

McKenna, David L. *The Coming Great Awakening.* Downers Grove, IL: I.V.P., 1990. The role of youth in past spiritual awakenings and the prospect of youth being on the vanguard of the next great spiritual awakening.

McLaughlin, William G. *Modern Revivalism: Charles G. Finny to Billy Graham.* New York: Ronald Press, 1959. This book analyzes the social history and value changes that characterize times of spiritual awakening. He is somewhat critical in his analysis of revivalists.

Meeks Steve. *The Last Great Revival.* Houston: Calvary Publications, 1994. Contains some interesting prophetic insights from Scripture about the end-time revival.

Morgan, G. Campbell. *Lessons of the Welsh Revival (1904).* New York: Fleming H. Revell, 1905.

Murray, Andrew. *Revival*. Minneapolis: Bethany House, 1990.

Murphy, Owen; and Adams, John Wesley. *The Fire of God's Presence*. Kansas City, MO: Ambassadors Press, 2003. An account of the Hebrides Revival 1949-1953.

Murray, Iain. *Revival and Revivalism: The Making and Marriage of American Evangelicalism 1750- 1858*. Edinburgh: Banner of Truth, 1994.

Olford, Stephen F. *Lord Open the Heavens: A Heartcry for Revival*. Wheaton, IL: Harold Shaw, 1980.

Orr, J. Edwin. *Campus Aflame*. Glendale, CA: Gospel Light Publications, 1971.

Orr is the foremost historian and authority on revivals worldwide.

Orr, J. Edwin. *The Eager Feet: Evangelical Awakenings, 1790-1830*. Chicago: Moody Press, 1975.

Orr, J. Edwin. *Evangelical Awakenings*. 5 vols. Minneapolis: Bethany House, 1975, 1976, 1978.

Orr, J. Edwin. *The Fervent Prayer: The Worldwide Impact of the Great Awakening of 1858*. Chicago: Moody Press, 1974.

Orr, J. Edwin. *The Flaming Tongue: The Impact of the Twentieth Century Revivals*. Chicago: Moody Press, 1973.

Orr, J. Edwin. *The Second Evangelical Awakening in America*. London: Marshall, Morgan, and Scott. 1952.

Pratney, Winkie. *Revival: Principles to Change the World*. Springdale, PA: Whitaker House, 1983. A good overview of the history of revivals, with astute observations about enduring revival principles.

Ravenhill, Leonard. *Revival God's Way*. Minneapolis: Bethany House, 1983. Rejects shallow and superficial answers to the church's lack of power. Prophetic call for the church to return to her source of power.

Ravenhill, Leonard. *Revival Praying*. Minneapolis: Bethany House, 1962. A series of inspiring exhortations on the importance of prayer leading to revival.

Ravenhill, Leonard. *Why Revival Tarries*. Minneapolis: Bethany Fellowship, 1959. This is Ravenhill's first book and most popular one.

Riss, Richard M. *A Survey of 20th Century Revival Movements in North America*. Peabody, MA: Hendrickson Publishers, 1988. An excellent little handbook on 20th century revivals in America.

Riss Richard M. and Kathryn . *Images of Revival*. Shippensburg, PA: Destiny Image, 1998.

Robeck, Cecil M. Jr. *Azusa Street Mission & Revival: Birth of the Global Pentecost Movement.* Nashville: Nelson, 2006.

Sherrill, John L. *They Speak with Other Tongues.* New York: Pyramid Books, 1964. A popular and worthwhile book that describes the role of tongues in the Pentecostal and Charismatic revivals.

Smith, Timothy L. *Revivalism and Social Reform: American Protestantism on the Eve of the Civil War.* Nashville: Abingdon Press, 1957. This is an award winning volume in the field of history that documents the social reforms that resulted from the 19th century American revivals.

Snyder, Howard A. *The Divided Flame: Wesleyans and the Charismatic Revival.* Downers Grove, IL: I.V.F. Press, 1986. Notes the common heritage but separate paths that have been taken by two groups in Christendom because of the tongues and prophecy issues.

Steward, James A. *Invasion of Wales by the Spirit Through Evan Roberts.* Asheville, NC: Revival Literature, n.d.

Stibbe, Mark. *Revival.* East Sussex, England: Monarch Books, 1998. Vicar of St. Andrews Chorleywood, David Pytches successor. A timely reminder that revival involves both God's sovereignty and the church's responsibility, unusual manifestations and the conversion of the lost to Christ. ,

Stibbe, Mark. *Times of Refreshing: A Practical Theology of Revival for Today.* London: Marshall Pickering, 1995.

Sweet, William Warren. *Revivalism in America.* Nashville: Abingdon Press, 1944.

Synan, Vinson. *The Holiness-Pentecostal Movement in the United States.* Grand Rapids: Eerdmans, 1971. A solid historical account of the early developments of the holiness and Pentecostal movements.

Synan, Vinson. *In the Latter Days: The Outpouring of the Holy Spirit in the Twentieth Century.* Ann Arbor, MI: Servant Books, 1984. A brief account of the Pentecostal revival world-wide up to 1984.

Towns, Elmer and Porter, Douglas. *The Ten Greatest Revivals Ever.* Ann Arbor, MI: Vine Books, 2000.

Wagner, C. Peter. *Spiritual Power and Church Growth.* Altamonte Springs, FL: Strang Communications, 1986. Describes the ongoing revival growth of Pentecostal churches in Latin America.

Wagner, C. Peter. *Revival: It Can Transform Your City.* Colorado Springs: Wagner Institute, 2000.

Wallis, Arthur. *Revival: The Rain from Heaven.* Old Tappan, NJ: Fleming H. Revell, 1979. A superb book that examines the true purpose,

characteristics, and results of revival. Written by a 20th century Eng-
lishman who has led the way in the English restoration movement.

White, John. *When the Spirit Comes with Power: Signs and Wonders Among
God's People*. Downers Grove, IL: I.V.F. Press, 1988. A Spirit-filled
Canadian psychiatrist and pastor examines a variety of physical and
emotional manifestations that can accompany revival.

Whittaker, Colin C. *Great Revivals*. Springfield, MO: Radiant Books,
1984. Brief accounts of revivals in the 18th, 19th and 20th centuries.

DVD Material on Revival

"A Diary of Revival" About Evan Roberts and the Welsh Revival. www.
visionvideo.com

"A Revival Account: Asbury – 1970." Asbury College Revival, February,
1970.

"The Azusa Street Project." www.TheAzusaStreetProject.com

"God's Generals." 12 volume DVD set.

Orr, J. Edwin. *"The Role of Prayer in Spiritual Awakenings."* An inspiring
lecture by the foremost historian of revivals. www.go2rpi.com

Otis, George, Jr. Transformation DVDs. The Sentinel Group. www.
TransformNations.com

"Transformations I, II." Communities in the world that have experienced
transforming revival.

"Let the Sea Resound." About transformation on the islands of Fiji.

"An Unconventional War". Transformation documentary featuring
Uganda

"The Quickening." Principles of and obstacles to transforming revival.

"An Appalachian Dawn". Transformation story featuring Manchester, Kentucky

About Fusion Ministries

Fusion Ministries is dedicated to the pursuit of God's presence and glory becoming a tangible reality in both individual lives and entire communities. We serve as a catalyst to ignite fire for revival and hope for supernatural, presence-based transformation.

The primary emphasis of the ministry is to provide inspiration, consultation and teaching Biblical principles from God's word to encourage the citywide church to prepare for the habitation of God's presence, unto transforming revival.

Fusion Ministries is called to serve as a "bridge" to connect three important realities of the Kingdom of God: the call to intimacy with Jesus, the vision of transforming revival, and the mandate to take that message to the nations.

If you would like additional information about our ministry please contact us:

Fusion Ministries, Inc.
721 Main Street, Suite #105
Grandview, MO 64030
(816) 965-5470

Info@fusionministry.com
www.fusionministry.com

Other Resources From Fusion Ministries

"Desperate for His Presence" - Rhonda Hughey $14

Are you tired of church as usual? Hungry for more? This book will encourage you to pursue the manifest presence of God unto transformation of your own heart, your family, congregation and community!

"The Fire of God's Presence" - Dr. Wes Adams $9

Documenting the powerful transforming revival that occurred in the Hebrides Islands, this book, filled with first-hand accounts, will stir your heart with faith for revival in our generation!

"PURITY" - Rhonda Hughey & Wes Adams $6

This booklet brings much needed clarity for believers regarding sexual purity so they can contend for right-eousness in a culture filled with compromise!

"The Divine Experiment" - Rhonda Hughey & Wes Adams

The "Divine Experiment" is a radical, corporate 21-day fast from the status quo. It is a time of consecration to the Lord as individuals, families and congregations. Prayer guide is not available for sale but is made available to communities who commit to the consecration process.

For more information on Fusion Ministries, or other resources please contact us: www.fusionministry.com